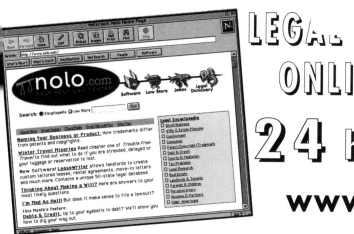

# Personal Record Keeper

5

Windows & Macintosh

## Users' Manual

by Albin Renauer & Ely Newman

## KEEPING UP TO DATE

To keep its books up to date, Nolo issues new printings and new editions periodically. New printings reflect minor legal changes and technical corrections. New editions contain major legal changes, major text additions or major reorganizations. To find out if a later printing or edition of any Nolo book is available, call Nolo at 510-549-1976 or check our website: www.nolo.com.

To stay current, follow the "Update" service at our website: www.nolo.com. In another effort to help you use Nolo's latest materials, we offer a 35% discount off the purchase of the new edition of your Nolo book when you turn in the cover of an earlier edition.
This manual was last revised in October 1998.

**Fifth Edition**

| | |
|---|---|
| *First Printing* | **OCTOBER 1998** |
| *Conceptual Design* | Albin Renauer, Carol Pladsen & Ralph Warner |
| *Software Development* | Flashpoint, Inc., Albin Renauer, Natalie DeJarlais, Jenya Chernoff, Allen Santos, Michael Sexton |
| *Documentation* | Albin Renauer & Ely Newman |
| *Production* | Ely Newman & Allen Santos |
| *Book design* | Albin Renauer |
| *Box/Cover design* | Linda M. Wanczyk |
| *Proofreading* | Robert Wells |
| *Index* | Nancy Mulvany |
| *Printing* | Bertelsmann Industry Services, Inc. |

*Quicken* is a registered trademark of Intuit Corporation.

*Apple* and *Macintosh* are registered trademarks of Apple Computer Company, Inc.

Renauer, Albin.
      Personal recordKeeper : version 5 / by Albin Renauer.
         p.  cm.
      Includes index.
      ISBN 0-87337-483-5
      1. Personal recordkeeper.  2.  Finance, Personal--Computer
      programs.  3.  Records--Management--Computer programs.  I. Title.
      HG179.R3933  1998
      640'.285'5369--dc21                            98-16995
                                                  CIP

## ACKNOWLEDGMENTS

Without the patience and hard work of programmers and designers at Flashpoint, Inc. (Eric Levine, Stephen Zeik, Roger Willson, David Schulman, Bill Dougherty, Peter Chestena), Michael Sexton of GloriaSoft, and especially Nolo Press editor Albin Renauer, who conscientiously and creatively edited the manual and software and designed the 5th version, Personal RecordKeeper would not be in your hands. Thanks to all for making Personal RecordKeeper 5.0 real.

A number of other people gave generously of their good ideas, creative suggestions and bug swatting skills. We appreciate the help of Jenya Chernoff, Natalie DeJarlais, Susan Cornell, Ann Heron, Amina Inloes, Ely Newman, Mary Randolph, Mark Stuhr, Bob Cosby, Jeff Brascher and Allen Santos. Sincere thanks to all other Noloids, past and present, who worked on previous versions of the program.

Other people at Nolo will become more involved now that Personal RecordKeeper 5 is on the market. We'd like to thank them all in advance.

## ABOUT NOLO PRESS

### The leading publisher of self-help law books and software since 1971

Nolo Press was founded in 1971 to show people how to do their own routine legal tasks and avoid costly lawyer fees. Early on, bar associations thundered against self-help law, claiming that lawyers were essential to help with even simple legal procedures. But Nolo persisted, sure that informed people armed with top-quality self-help information did not have to depend on lawyers. Over the years, more than three million customers have proven us right. Today, Nolo publishes over 100 self-help law books, audio tapes, videos and software packages—and is more committed than ever to making the law accessible.

This is a software license agreement between Nolo Press and you as purchaser, for the use of the Personal RecordKeeper program and accompanying manual. By using this program and manual, you indicate that you accept all terms of this agreement. If you do not agree to all the terms and conditions of this agreement, do not use the Personal RecordKeeper program or manual, but return both to Nolo Press for a full refund.

### Grant of License

In consideration of payment of the license fee, which is part of the price you paid for Personal RecordKeeper, Nolo Press as licensor grants to you the right to use the enclosed program for yourself and your immediate family, subject to the terms and restrictions set forth in this license agreement.

### Copy, Use and Transfer Restrictions

The Personal RecordKeeper manual and the program and its documentation are copyrighted. You may not give, sell or otherwise distribute copies of the program to third parties, except as provided in the U.S. Copyright Act. Under this license agreement, you may not use the program for commercial or nonprofit purposes.

### Commercial Use of This Product

This product may not be used commercially. It is intended for personal use only.

### Disclaimer of Warranty and Limited Warranty

This program and accompanying manual are sold "AS IS," without any implied or express warranty as to their performance or to the results that may be obtained by using the program.

As to the original purchaser only, Nolo Press warrants that the magnetic or optional disk on which the program is recorded shall be free from defects in material and workmanship in normal use and service. If a defect in this disk occurs, the disk may be returned to Nolo Press. We will replace the disk free of charge. In the event of a defect, your exclusive remedy is expressly limited to replacement of the disk as described above.

## Your Responsibilities for Your Documents

Although best efforts were devoted to making this material useful, accurate and up to date, we have no control over whether you carefully follow our instructions or properly understand the information in the Personal RecordKeeper disk or manual.

Of necessity, therefore, Nolo Press does not make any guarantees about the use to which the software or manual are put, or the results of that use.

## Term

The license is in effect until terminated. You may terminate it at any time by destroying the program together with all copies and modifications in any form.

## Entire Agreement

By using the Personal RecordKeeper program, you agree that this license is the complete and exclusive statement of the agreement between you and Nolo Press regarding Personal RecordKeeper.

# Table of Contents

# Table of Contents

# Table of Contents

# Chapter 1.   Introduction

Welcome to *Personal RecordKeeper*, the most useful and thorough record keeping software available. This manual explains how to use *Personal RecordKeeper*.

In this chapter, you'll learn how this manual is organized and where to find the information you need.

Be sure to read the Read Me file contained on your *Personal RecordKeeper* disk for information that did not make it into this manual.

## What's in this manual?

Here's a summary of how this manual is organized:

- **Chapter 1: Introduction.** Overview of the manual, glossary, explanation of icons used in the manual, and a list of new features found in this version of *Personal RecordKeeper*.

- **Chapter 2: Installing and Starting *Personal RecordKeeper*.** How to install and start *Personal RecordKeeper* and create your first database file.

- **Chapter 3: Overview of *Personal RecordKeeper*.** An overview of what *Personal RecordKeeper* is, how it works, and what the different parts of its screen are for.

- **Chapter 4: Entering and Saving Information.** How to find the right Category and Subcategory for your information. How to create new Entries within a Subcategory. How to use multi-screen (tabbed) Entries. How to add comments (Notes) to any Entry. How to modify the Location and Insurance lists that appear in Category 10.

- **Chapter 5: Using the Names List.** How to enter names, in general, how to paste in a name that you've already entered, how to edit the Names List, and how to import names from other applications.

- **Chapter 6: Organizing and Retrieving Your Information.** How to sort Entries within each Subcategory and how to use the Find feature to locate text anywhere in your database.

- **Chapter 7: Creating and Printing Reports.** How to view, format and print various kinds of reports of information you have entered, and how to print blank worksheets.

- **Chapter 8: Exporting Information to Other Applications.** How to export *Personal RecordKeeper's* reports to other applications, and how to export information to a tab- or comma-separated plain text (ASCII) file.

- **Chapter 9: Locking Your Data.** How to use *Personal RecordKeeper's* password protection to keep your information private.

- **Chapter 10: Customizing *Personal RecordKeeper.*** How to change the default settings of *Personal RecordKeeper's* basic operations, and how to change the user name of the current database.

- **Chapter 11: Troubleshooting**. Information about problems you may encounter when using *Personal RecordKeeper* and how to contact Nolo Press Technical Support, as well as specifications for the software.

- **Appendices**
  - Appendix A.  Complete List of Categories and Subcategories
  - Appendix B.  What's Included in Net Worth Reports
  - Appendix C.  Formats for Entering Dates
  - Appendix D.  Keyboard Shortcuts
  - Appendix E.  Examples of Exported Subcategory Data

- **Index**. The index for this manual.

## The Read Me file

The *Personal RecordKeeper* CD-ROM includes a Read Me file containing additional information that did not make it into this manual. Be sure to read this before you use the software.

To display the contents of this file on your screen, double-click the Read Me icon. Once the document is opened, you can print it by choosing Print from the File menu.

# What's new in version 5.0

Users who are upgrading from earlier versions will notice several significant new features:

### *Improved Handling of Names and Addresses*

- Names and addresses in your *RecordKeeper* database are now kept in a separate, reusable Names List. This means that once you type in a new name, you'll never have to retype it—you can reuse it any time by selecting it from the pop-up list that appears in every name field. You can also attach address, phone and e-mail information about each person or business, and call up this additional information anywhere you use the name in your database.

- Version 5 now lets you enter more information about each name. In addition to day and evening phone numbers for each person and a contact person for each business, you can now include e-mail addresses, FAX numbers, pager numbers and URLs. And, because this information is stored globally in the Names List, any change you make to this needs to be made only once—the updated information will appear wherever that name is used in the database.

### *Importing Names and Addresses*

If you use an address book program or personal information manager (PIM) to keep track of business and personal contacts on your computer, you can import all this information directly into your *RecordKeeper* database. This gives you a head start in entering your information as well as a complete record of how those businesses and individuals are relevant in your life and business.

### *Seamless Integration with Nolo Press's* **WillMaker 7**

- If you are a *WillMaker 7* user, you'll be able to use that program to browse relevant *RecordKeeper* information and enter and update the information that appears in the "Personal Records" worksheets. See your *WillMaker 7* manual for more information on how to use *Personal RecordKeeper 5* to generate and update Personal Records worksheets.

- If you've already created documents with *WillMaker 7*, you can export all the name and address information from your *WillMaker* portfolio into your *RecordKeeper* database.

### *New and Revised Subcategories*

- In Category 3,. Current Income, there's a place to enter information about long-term disability income.

- In Category 5, Securities, there's a place to enter information about Brokerage Accounts as well as separate subcategories for Corporate and Municipal Bonds.

- In Category 10, Home Inventory, there's now a field in each Subcategory to indicate whether the item is individually or jointly owned and a field to enter the name of the co-owners (if the item is jointly owned).

  If you are upgrading from *PRK* version 4.0 and converting a version 4 data file, be sure to go over each Entry in this Category and enter the correct ownership information.

- In Category 13, People/Services, there are new Subcategories for Subscriptions of any kind and Memberships in health clubs, book clubs, or any other kind of organization.

### *Over 100 new fields throughout the database*

We've added over 100 new data entry fields throughout, so that *PRK* can do an even more thorough job of recording and organizing your personal information. If you're upgrading from a previous version and have converted your data file (see Chapter 2), take the time to review your existing Entries to see where you can enter information into new fields.

## System requirements

### Windows

- 486 or higher IBM PC (Pentium preferred) or compatible, with at least 8 MB of RAM (Random Access Memory)

- 8 MB free disk space, 14 MB to install

- Printer (to print out your final documents)

- Microsoft Windows 95 or later

- CD-ROM drive (for installation).

### Macintosh

- Macintosh or compatible computer with a 68030 processor or greater

- 8 MB of RAM (Random Access Memory), with 4MB free

- 9MB free disk space, 16 to install

- Printer (to print out database reports)

- System 7.0 or later

- CD-ROM drive (for installation).

---

**If you need to install from floppy disks**

If you are a registered user and would prefer to install the program from 3-1/2" floppy disks, contact Nolo Press Customer Service:

- call:     800-992-6656

- e-mail:  cs@nolo.com

- fax:     510-548-5902

There will be a small fee to cover shipping and handling.

---

## Special information for Macintosh users

This Users' Guide is for both Windows and Macintosh users. We have designed *Personal RecordKeeper 5* so that it is virtually identical for both platforms. For this reason, we can use illustrations ("screen shots") from the Windows version that apply to the Mac version as well.

Wherever the Windows and Mac versions differ significantly, we include special instructions for Mac users.

---

**The Macintosh Command Key**

Throughout the manual, you'll find references to the Command key. This is the key with the "Apple" icon to the left of the Space bar on your keyboard. Mac users should use the Command key instead of the Ctrl key found on Windows computers.

---

## Register your copy

Registered owners of Nolo products receive a variety of free services and benefits.

But to provide these services, we need to know who you are. Please take the time now to complete and mail the registration card. You'll find it in the package this product came in. If you purchased this program directly from Nolo Press, you are already registered and needn't send in the card.

We also would appreciate any comments you have on our product. We read every comment on every registration card.

## The *Nolo News*

As a registered user of a Nolo Press product, you will receive a free, one-year subscription to the *Nolo News*, our quarterly publication.

The *Nolo News* contains:

- articles on estate planning, consumer law, personal finance, small business law and other topics of interest
- the latest product news
- Nolo's famous lawyer jokes column, and
- a complete catalog of all our books and software.

If you buy other Nolo products or upgrade this product in the two-year period, you get another year free. If your free period runs out, another one-year subscription costs $10.

## Terminology used in this manual

Here are a few terms used to describe the various parts of *Personal RecordKeeper*.

- **Category:** A group of Subcategory topics that organize your data into logical groups. There are 27 Categories in *Personal RecordKeeper*. They are displayed in the upper left pane of the application window. A complete list of Categories and Subcategories can be found in Appendix A. See Chapter 3 for a more detailed discussion.

- **Category Group:** A group of Categories that appear as folders in the top left pane of the application window. There are six Category Group folders that you can expand or contract to display the Categories within them. See Chapter 3 for a more detailed discussion.

- **Data Screens:** The pre-designed screens that make up each Entry.

- **Database, Database File or Data File:** These terms are used interchangeably. They all refer to the file you create that holds your *Personal RecordKeeper* data.

- **Entries:** The sets of information that you record within each Subcategory. When you open a Subcategory, you are presented with a pre-designed, fill-in-the-blanks screen or series of data screens. When you fill in these blanks, you are creating a single "Entry." You can create an unlimited number of Entries in any Subcategory by choosing the New Entry command in the Entry menu.

- **Pane:** One of the three portions of the *Personal RecordKeeper* application window.

- **PRK:** An abbreviation for the name of this product, *Personal RecordKeeper*.

- **Prompt:** The title or name that appears before each field on a data screen, and on database printouts.

- **Subcategory:** A topic within a Category. Subcategories for each Category are displayed in the lower left pane of the application window, and in Appendix A of this manual. Each Subcategory can hold an unlimited number of Entries, as long as you have hard disk space available.

## Icons used in this manual

Especially important or useful information in this manual is flagged this way:

 WARNING! Indicates something that may cause you to lose data unexpectedly. Be sure to read all warnings in this manual very carefully.

 IMPORTANT! Indicates information that is fundamental to your understanding of how *Personal RecordKeeper* operates. This icon is used especially to point out aspects of the program that may not be immediately obvious.

 TIPS: Makes suggestions that will enhance your productivity with *Personal RecordKeeper*. They flag time-saving techniques, point out easier ways to accomplish a desired task, explain a feature more fully or point out possible uses of a feature that may not be immediately obvious.

 NOTES: Provides additional information about a subject that may be helpful to certain kinds of users.

# Chapter 2.  Installing and Starting
## *Personal RecordKeeper*

*Installing Personal RecordKeeper*

*Starting Personal RecordKeeper*

*After you start up Personal RecordKeeper*

*Converting version 4.0 or 3.0 database files*

*After a database file is open*


## Installing *Personal RecordKeeper*

You will need approximately 14 MB of free space (16 MB if you're using a Mac) on your hard disk to install *Personal RecordKeeper* 5 and its accompanying help files.

### Windows

Step 1.     Start your computer.

Step 2.     Insert the *Personal RecordKeeper* CD into your CD-ROM drive.

Step 3.     Follow the instructions that appear on the screen.

### Macintosh

Step 1.     Start up your Macintosh.

Step 2.     Insert the *Personal RecordKeeper* CD into your CD-ROM drive.

Step 3.     Double-click the *Personal RecordKeeper 5* Installer icon.

Step 4.     Follow the instructions that appear on the screen.

---

**If you are upgrading from *Personal RecordKeeper* 4.0 or 3.0.**

Databases created with version 4.0 (Windows or Macintosh) or with version 3.0 (DOS or Macintosh) can be converted for use in *Personal RecordKeeper5*. However, do not remove your earlier version of *Personal RecordKeeper* until you have successfully converted your old database. If there is a problem with your 3.0 database file, you may have to fix the problem with version 3.0 before you convert, as discussed later in this chapter.

---

### Read the Read Me file

The *Personal RecordKeeper* folder that's created upon installation contains a Read Me file. Open the Read Me file to see important information that didn't make it into this manual. You should read this file *before* you start up *Personal RecordKeeper*.

## Starting *Personal RecordKeeper*

Once you've installed *Personal RecordKeeper* on your hard disk, you're ready to start the program.

### Windows

Step 1.    Click the Start button in the Windows 95 task bar.

Step 2.    Point to Programs to open the Programs folder.

Step 3.    Point to *Personal RecordKeeper 5* to open the *Personal RecordKeeper 5* application folder.

Step 4.    Click the *Personal RecordKeeper* application icon.

### Macintosh

Step 1.    Find and open the *Personal RecordKeeper 5* folder.

Step 2.    Double-click the *Personal RecordKeeper 5* application icon.

## After you start up *Personal RecordKeeper*

Whenever you start *Personal RecordKeeper*, the last database you had opened will be reopened automatically. If you are using the program for the first time, you will instead see the Welcome screen.

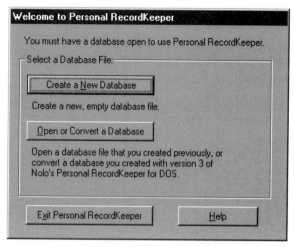

*The Welcome screen appears the first time you start Personal RecordKeeper.*

The Welcome screen offers the following choices:

- **Create a New Database.** Click this button to create a new, empty database file.

- **Open or Convert a Database.** Click this button to open a database that you already created with this version of *Personal RecordKeeper*, or to convert a database you created with *Personal RecordKeeper* version 3 or 4. See below for complete instructions.

- **Help.** Click this button to learn how to operate this part of *Personal RecordKeeper*, as well as access to an online version of the entire *Personal RecordKeeper* manual.

- **Exit *Personal RecordKeeper*.** Click this button to quit the program.

## Creating a new database file

To create a new database file:

- Click the New Database button on the Welcome screen described above, or

- If *Personal RecordKeeper* is already running and using a different database, choose New Database from the File menu.

When you create a new database, you are first asked for the name of the person whose records will be kept in this file.

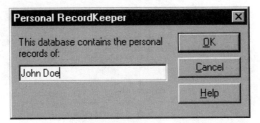

*When you create a database, you enter the name
of the person whose records will be stored in it.*

The name you type will appear in the status bar at the bottom left of the application window whenever you use this file. It will also appear in the footer and Title Page of all reports you print. Enter the name and click OK.

You can change this name at any time by selecting the Settings command in the Options menu. (See Chapter 10, *Customizing Personal Record Keeper*.)

Next, a dialog box will appear asking you to name and save the file. To accept the default name (see *The name of your version 5 database file*, below), just click Save.

## The name of your version 5 database file

### *Windows*

After you enter your name, the newly-created database file is the first eight characters of your first name with the three-letter extension PR5 at the end.

EXAMPLE: Mary Jones creates a database and types "Mary Jones" in the first dialog box. In the Create a Personal RecordKeeper Database dialog, her file is assigned the default name MARY.PR5, which she accepts by clicking Save. Now, whenever this database file is opened the status bar at the bottom of the application window says "Mary Jones" and the title bar says MARY.PR5.

Windows 95 users can change the file name to a longer one of up to 32 characters. Do NOT, however, change the three-character extension PR5 at the end.

### *Macintosh*

After you enter your name, the newly-created database file is your full name, plus "'s Records."

EXAMPLE: Mary Jones creates a database and types "Mary Jones" in the first dialog box. In the Create a Personal RecordKeeper Database dialog, her file is assigned the default name MARY JONES'S RECORDS, which she accepts by clicking Save Now, whenever this database file is opened the status bar at the bottom of the application window says "Mary Jones" and the title bar says MARY JONES'S RECORDS.

## Opening a file created with *Personal RecordKeeper 5*

To open a database file created with *Personal RecordKeeper* version 5:

*   Click the Open Database button on the Welcome screen when you first start the program (described earlier), or

*   If *Personal RecordKeeper* is already running and using a different database, choose Open Database from the File menu.

A standard open dialog box will appear, listing all *Personal RecordKeeper 5.0* database files in the current folder.

*The Open a Personal RecordKeeper Database dialog box.*

Double-click on the file you want, or select it and click the OK button. If the file was created with an earlier version of *Personal RecordKeeper*, you will need to convert the database file as described below.

## Converting version 4.0 or 3.0 database files

*Personal RecordKeeper* 5.0 can open database files created with version 4.0 (Windows or Macintosh) and version 3.0 ( DOS and Macintosh), but you must convert the older-version database to the version 5 format.

 CONVERTING FILES FROM VERSION 3.0 FOR DOS: If you want to convert a database from *Nolo's Personal RecordKeeper* 3.0 for DOS, read the section *Preparing to convert a file created with version 3.0 for DOS*, below.

Step 1.    Choose one of the following methods:

- If you are running version 5 for the first time, click the Open or Convert button at the Welcome screen (described earlier), or

- If *Personal RecordKeeper* is already running and another database is open, choose Convert from the File menu, or

- If *Personal RecordKeeper* is already running and another database is open, choose Open from the File menu.

Step 2.    This step varies depending on which option you used in Step 1:

- If you clicked Open or Convert on the Welcome screen or selected Open from the File menu, a standard Open dialog appears. Locate and select the database file you want to convert, then click OK.

- If you selected Convert from the File menu, a Convert Database dialog appears. Locate and select the database file you want to convert, then click OK.

- If you selected Open from the File menu, go on to Step 3.

Step 3.    Next, the Incorrect Version dialog box appears asking if you want to convert the older-version file. Click Convert.

Step 4.    You'll then see the Create a Personal RecordKeeper Database dialog. To accept the default name and convert the file, click Save.

**Locating database files from older versions of *Personal RecordKeeper***

**Version 4 for Windows:** By default this program is installed in the \NPR4 directory. Version 4 database files have the extension PRK.

**Version 4 for Macintosh:** By default this program is installed in the *Personal RecordKeeper* folder. Version 4 database files include your full name, followed by " 's Records".

**Version 3 for Macintosh:** By default this program is installed in the *NPR Program* folder. Version 3 database files include your first name, followed by " 's Database".

**Version 3 for DOS:** By default this program is installed in the \NPR directory. Version 3 database files are eight-characters without a three-letter extension at the end.

RESOLVING CONFLICTS IN THE NAMES LIST: When you convert data from a previous version, *PRK* goes through each record, and prompts you to resolve all conflicts (for example, if you have two different phone numbers for the same person). For details on what to do if you see the Names List Conflict dialog box, see *If RecordKeeper detects conflicts in Names List data*, below.

When the conversion process is complete, the newly created version 5 database file is open. Be sure to go through the database to make sure that the conversion was successful and to clean up data in the Names List, if necessary (see Chapter 5, *Using the Names List*).

## If *RecordKeeper* detects conflicts in Names List data

As will be discussed in detail in Chapter 5, a new Names List feature has been added to help organize information about all persons, organizations and business entities named in your database. When you convert an existing database created with an older version of *PRK*, the program "reads" each record looking for conflicting Names List information. If a conflict is found, you'll see the Names List Conflict dialog box.

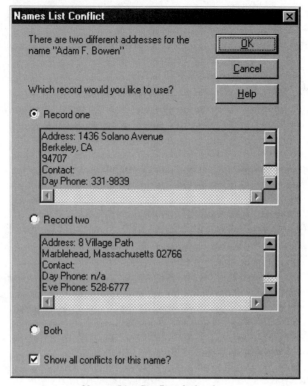

*Names List Conflict dialog box*

To resolve a conflict using the Names List Conflict dialog box:

Step 1.  Read the first line to see what the conflict is—for example, different addresses, different phone numbers, etc.

Step 2.  Compare *all* the data in Record 1 with that in Record 2.

Step 3.  Select which record you want to include in your database.

- If you want to include only the data in Record 1, click **Record 1**.

- If you want to include only the data in Record 2, click **Record 2**.

- If both Record 1 and Record 2 contain data you want to keep (for example, Record 1 has John Smith's home phone number and record 2 has his work number), click **Combine information into one record**.

  Be aware that if you make this selection, the newly created record contains *all the data in both records*. For example,

  - If the two records have *different* phone numbers, *both will be included* in the new combined record.

- If two records have the *same* phone number, *this number will show up twice* in the new combined record.

When the conversion is completed, you will be able to clean up the data and get rid of any unwanted duplication (see *Modifying names and adding information* in Chapter 5).

Whatever selection you make will appear as Record 1 in this dialog box when any additional conflicts for this name are shown.

Step 4.    Select whether you want to keep viewing other conflicting records for the same name.

If the record you selected has the correct, complete information, there's no need to view other conflicting records; in this case, you can safely uncheck the box.

Step 5.    Click OK.

When you've completed this process, and especially if you've combined data from conflicting records, we recommend that you immediately open the Names List to review your data and clean up any duplicate data, if necessary. For details on how to do this, see *Modifying names and adding information* Chapter 5.

## Preparing to convert a file created with version 3.0 for DOS

Before trying to convert database files created with version 3 of *Nolo's Personal RecordKeeper* for DOS (*NPR*), you need to "prepare" the file by quitting *Personal RecordKeeper 5* (if it's open) and completing the following steps.

Step 1.    Start *NPR* version 3 for DOS. As the program starts, note the version number displayed on the initial screen and jot it down. You may need this information later. If your version 3 file does not open automatically, open it by choosing Load from the File menu. When the open dialog appears, type in the full path of the file where your records are stored in *NPR*.

Step 2.    Write down the full path name of your file. You can find the full path name of your file displayed on the Main Menu, just below the subcategory. For example, the full path name of your file might be C:\NPR\JOANNE.

Step 3.    Run the automatic corruption fixer in version 3 for DOS. While at the Main Menu, and with your file open, hold down the Ctrl and Alt keys while pressing the hyphen key. (The hyphen key is next to the number "0" at the top of your keyboard.) This will cause NPR DOS to scan your database and fix any corruption it finds. If corruption is detected, note the sections that are mentioned. The data in these sections may be incomplete or deleted.

Step 4.     Choose Save a Copy from the File menu to save a copy of your database with a different name. This may take a while. This command saves the database in a form that is more efficient for conversion. This is the file you will convert for use in version 5, so take note of its full path and name.

Step 5.     Choose the Save a Copy command again, this time saving your file to a floppy diskette or to a different directory on your hard drive. This file is for safekeeping, just in case you experience any conversion difficulties.

Step 6.     Quit *NPR* version 3.0 and start Windows.

Now you're ready to actually do the conversion as explained at the beginning of this section.

## If *Personal RecordKeeper* detects corruption in your version 3 file

Before *Personal RecordKeeper* attempts to convert your version 3 database file, it does a complete scan for any signs of corruption. It is possible that over years of use, your database created with *Personal RecordKeeper* version 3 has become corrupted in some minor way. You may well have never noticed this corruption, because the affected part of the database hadn't been used for many months or years. However, the thorough scan of the database will detect this corruption when you attempt to convert.

If corruption is detected, you will receive a message informing you of the problem. Here is what you need to do to fix the corruption (have a pen or pencil and paper handy):

### *If your version 3.0 for DOS file is corrupt*

Step 1.     Start *Nolos Personal RecordKeeper* version 3 for DOS (*NPR*) and Load your database (choose Load from the File menu). For detailed instructions on loading a database, please refer to Chapter 5 in the *NPR* version 3 User's Guide.

*NPR* will open, and after a few seconds you'll see the Main Menu showing Categories and Subcategories.

Step 2. Press the Ctrl and the Alt keys simultaneously, holding them down while you tap the Hyphen (Dash or Minus) key once. Release all the keys. This will start a "Scan and Repair" of the database.

Step 3. As the database is scanning, you may get a message that reads:

**"Found damage in (cat./sub cat.) some data may be lost... press any key."**

Write down the location of the damage. Press any key to continue. There may be more than one error found. Once the scan is complete, repeat step 3 until no errors are found.

Step 4. Go to the File menu (Alt+F) and select Save Copy. A dialog box will appear asking you to enter a database name. If the original name of your database was "Items," for example, you could call the new one "Items2." Press Enter. The words "Writing Database" should appear at the bottom left of the screen.

Step 5. Exit *NPR* version 3 by choosing Exit from the File menu.

Step 6. Restart *Personal RecordKeeper* version 5.

Step 7. Choose the Convert command from the File menu and select the database you just repaired. The file should convert successfully.

If taking these steps does not fix the problem, read the READ ME file that came with *Personal RecordKeeper* version 5 for further instructions.

### *If your version 3.0 for Mac file is corrupt*

Step 1. Quit *Personal RecordKeeper* version 5 by choosing Quit from the File menu.

Step 2. Start *Nolo's Personal RecordKeeper* version 3 for Macintosh.

Step 3. You'll see an open file dialog box. Find the version 3 database file where corruption was detected and click ONCE on it. Do *not* open it yet.

Step 4. While pressing the Option key on your keyboard, click the Open button. This will start a "Scan and Repair" of the selected database.

Step 5. When this process is complete, you'll see a message that the database has been repaired. Click OK.

Step 6. Quit *NPR* version 3 by choosing Quit from the File menu.

Step 7. Restart *Personal RecordKeeper* version 5.

Step 8.    Choose the Convert command from the File menu and select the database you just repaired. The file should convert successfully.

If taking these steps does not fix the problem, read the READ ME file that came with *Personal RecordKeeper* version 5 for further instructions.

## After you've successfully converted your database

Because of new features included in version 5, you need to review the converted database with respect to the (1) Names List and (2) Category 10, Home Ownership.

### *Reviewing information in the Names List*

If you resolved any Names List conflicts while converting your database (as discussed above), you'll need to open up the Names List to review it and, if necessary, clean it up. For details, see Chapter 5.

### *Indicating the form of ownership of items listed in Category 10, Home Inventory*

As discussed in Chapter 1, we've added an "Ownership is" field to all Subcategories in Category 10, Home Inventory. This field is used to indicate the form of ownership, or how an item of property is owned—individually, jointly, as community property, in joint tenancy, etc.

If you've converted a database created with a previous version of *PRK*, each Entry in Category 10 is assigned the default value of being individually owned. We strongly suggest that you review all Entries in this Category to verify and, if necessary, change the "Ownership is" information. This is especially important if you are married, since much of your personal property is likely to be co-owned, in some form, by your spouse.

## After a database file is open

Once a database is open, the main application window will be visible. Chapter 3 describes what to do next.

 TIP: When you first open your converted file (see *Converting version 4.0 or 3.0 database files*, above), we suggest you use *PRK* version 5.0's new Names List feature to add additional information about the persons, organizations and business entities listed in your database. See Chapter 5, *Using the Names List* to learn about the Names List.

# Chapter 3.  Overview of
# *Personal RecordKeeper*

OK, so you've started the program and created a database ... Now what? This chapter explains *Personal RecordKeeper's* design and purpose, and gives you some ideas on how to use it. It also provides a detailed tour of the application window, toolbar and menus, so you'll know about all the features at your disposal.

One thing to keep in mind as you start using *Personal RecordKeeper*: you won't fill up your database in a single evening—nor should you feel you must. Rome wasn't built in a day. A database with this amount of breadth can hold hundreds of pages of information. This is a "living" database, which you will change and update for many years to come. Start anywhere, fill in as much or as little as you like.

Don't feel obliged to use every Category of *Personal RecordKeeper*. It covers many different areas, some of which you may find more useful than others. But at least take the time to read this chapter to find out what's available, and then decide where you want to start.

Then take the time to browse through the Categories and Subcategories, and look at the kind of information you're asked to fill in on different screens. Chances are, you'll discover that you never realized how organized you could be, once you start using *Personal RecordKeeper*.

## How *Personal RecordKeeper* organizes your information

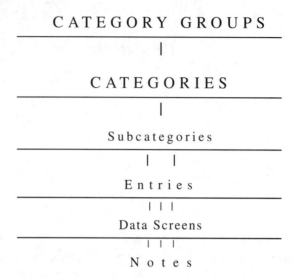

CATEGORY GROUPS

|

CATEGORIES

|

Subcategories

|  |

Entries

| | |

Data Screens

| | |

Notes

*Personal RecordKeeper* organizes your essential legal, practical and personal information into a pre-designed Category and Subcategory format.

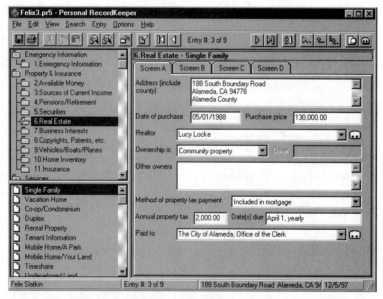

*The Personal RecordKeeper application window.*

*The Category pane (upper left) can be resized by clicking and dragging its bottom edge.*

## Category Groups and Categories

The top left pane of the application window lists *Personal RecordKeeper*'s 27 Categories, clustered into seven groups, described in the following table.

| | |
|---|---|
| **Vital Information. (Category 1):** Information that you or your loved ones are likely to need on short notice—for example, names of people to notify if there is an emergency. | 1. Emergency Information |
| **Property & Insurance. (Categories 2–11):** All kinds of property, including cash, pensions, IRAs, real estate, securities, cars, boats, household furnishings, other valuable objects, including collections of china, precious metals, animals or guns, and the insurance on these items. | 2. Available Money<br>3. Sources of Current Income<br>4. Pensions/Retirement<br>5. Securities<br>6. Real Estate<br>7. Business Interests<br>8. Copyrights, Patents, etc.<br>9. Vehicles/Boats/Planes<br>10. Home Inventory<br>11. Insurance |
| **Categories 12–13: Service Providers.** Persons you rely on for services, ranging from gardeners to stockbrokers to baby-sitters. | 12. Advisors–Money/Legal<br>13. People/Services |
| **Categories 14–17: Debts.** Debts you've paid, those you owe and those that people owe you. | 14. Tax Records<br>15. Credit Cards<br>16. What You Owe<br>17. What's Owed You |
| **Categories 18–20: Secured Places & Things.** Alarms, locks, keys and hiding places where you keep valuable or secret objects. | 18. Alarms<br>19. Locked Places/Keys<br>20. Hiding Places |
| **Categories 21–25: Personal Items & Biographical Information.** Personal documents (marriage certificates, passports, military records, etc.), memorabilia, and "vital statistics" about you and your family. Record these items for yourself and for future generations that may be interested in what life was like in the 20th century. | 21. Medical Information<br>22. Memorabilia<br>23. Personal Documents<br>24. Personal Information<br>25. Family Information |
| **Categories 26–27: Final Plans.** How you want your affairs handled at your death, including whether you want to donate organs, whether you want to be cremated and how you want your estate handled. (**Note:** Do not use this program as a substitute for a will. Use this program only to summarize what final plans you have already made.) | 26. Death Plans<br>27. Estate Planning |

### Category group icons

Clicking on a Category Group icon expands or collapses the folder.

### Category Icons

When you select a Category in the Category pane (located in the upper left of the main application window) its icon will change as follows:

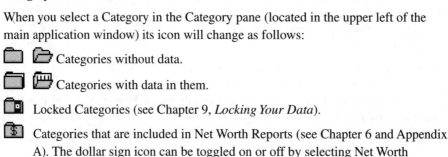

📁 📂 Categories without data.

📁 📂 Categories with data in them.

📁 Locked Categories (see Chapter 9, *Locking Your Data*).

💲 Categories that are included in Net Worth Reports (see Chapter 6 and Appendix A). The dollar sign icon can be toggled on or off by selecting Net Worth Indicators from the View menu.

💲 Categories that are locked and included in Net Worth Reports.

## Subcategories

When you click on a numbered Category, its Subcategories are listed in the Subcategory pane beneath the Category pane (located directly below the Category pane in the lower left of the main application window).

For example, the "Real Estate" Category is divided into your principal residence, your vacation home, your rental property and other Subcategories. (See the back of the manual for a complete list of Subcategories.) There are 230 Subcategories in *Personal RecordKeeper*. See Appendix A for a complete list.

### Subcategory Icons

📄 Subcategory has data. Until data is entered in the subcategory, no icon appears.

💲 Subcategory is included in Net Worth reports. The dollar sign indicator can be toggled on or off by selecting "Net Worth Indicators" from the View menu.

## Entries and Data Screens

Once you've selected a Subcategory, a fill-in-the-blanks "Entry" appears for that Subcategory. Each Subcategory has a unique Entry template for entering information. Some Subcategories' templates are made up of only one screen while other Subcategory templates consist of up to seven screens. These templates cannot be modified.

If the Subcategory you've chosen has a multiple-screen template, you'll see a series of tabs across the top. Click on the tabs to access each screen in that Subcategory.

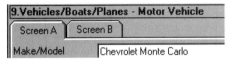

*Section of an Entry screen for Motor Vehicles in Category 9, Vehicles/Boats Planes.*

Each Subcategory's template is tailored to the type of information covered. For example, the Subcategory "Motor Vehicles" found in Category 9, Vehicles/ Boats/ Planes (above), has two screens (Screen A and Screen B) that prompt you for information about the make, model, ID number, license number, registered owner and financing of your vehicle.

Within each Subcategory you can create multiple Entries, limited only by the space on your hard disk. Create as many Entries as you need.

EXAMPLE: Felix Slatkin owns two cars, a Ford Taurus, and a Dodge Caravan. So Felix needs to create two Entries in the Subcategory "Motor Vehicles" in Category 9, Vehicles/Boats/Planes. First, he enters information about the Ford Taurus in Screens A, B and C of Entry # 1. Then he chooses New Entry from the Entry menu to create a second Entry. He then enters information about the Dodge Caravan in screens A, B and C of Entry #2. If Felix gets more cars, he can create more Entries at any time.

If you create more than one Entry within a Subcategory, you can navigate between entries by using the commands in the Entry menu or the buttons on the toolbar. You can also sort all Entries by any field on the screen. For detailed information about creating Entries, see Chapter 4, *Entering and Saving Information.* For information about sorting and searching information you've already entered, see Chapter 6, *Organizing and Retrieving Your Information.*

## Notes

Each Entry can include up to 30,000 characters of additional information by using a pop-up "Notes" dialog. Use the Notes feature to include information if you can't find a place for it anywhere else. For detailed information about creating Notes, see Chapter 4, *Entering and Saving Information.*

## The Toolbar

The Toolbar appears at the top of the *Personal RecordKeeper* application window, just below the menus. It can be shown or hidden by choosing Toolbar from the View menu. The Toolbar provides easy access to the most commonly used *Personal RecordKeeper* functions.

| Choose... | | To... |
| --- | --- | --- |
| | **Save** | Save the currently opened database to disk. |
| | **Print Report** | Print all or part of your Database. |
| | **Cut** | Move the currently selected text to the clipboard. |
| | **Copy** | Copy the currently selected text to the clipboard. |
| | **Paste** | Paste the clipboard contents at the current cursor location. |
| | **Find** | Search for any text within the database. |
| | **Find Again** | Repeat the last search request and continue to search. |
| | **Cross Reference** | List other Categories related to the current Category. |
| | **New Entry** | Create a new Entry in the current Subcategory. |
| | **First Entry** | Go to the first Entry in the current Subcategory, using the current sort order. |
| | **Previous Entry** | Go to the previous Entry in the current Subcategory, using the current sort order. |
| | **Next Entry** | Go to the next Entry in the current Subcategory, using the current sort order. |
| | **Last Entry** | Go to the last Entry in the current Subcategory, using the current sort order. |
| | **Sort By** | Set the field on which the Entries in the current Subcategory should be sorted. |
| | **Go To Entry** | List all Entries in the current Subcategory, and lets you choose a specific one. |

| Choose... | | To... |
|---|---|---|
| 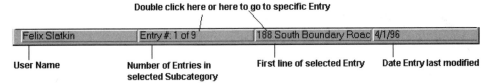 | **Go Back** | Go back to the most recent screens you have been viewing. |
| | **History** | List the last 40 screens you've viewed, and go directly to any of them. |
| | **Notes** | Add additional information to the current Entry |
| | **Names List** | Open the Names List of all persons, organizations or business entities in your database. Use the Names List to add names, enter additional personal information, or paste names into the current Entry. |

## The Status Bar

The Status bar, at the bottom of the application window, can be shown or hidden by choosing Status Bar from the View menu.

When a menu from the *Personal RecordKeeper* menu bar is selected, the Status Bar displays a short description of what the selected menu item does.

If no menu is selected, the Status Bar is split into four sections.

Double click here or here to go to specific Entry

| Felix Slatkin | Entry #: 1 of 9 | 188 South Boundary Road | 4/1/96 |

User Name    Number of Entries in    First line of selected Entry    Date Entry last modified
             selected Subcategory

*The Status Bar.*

The first section of the Status Bar on the left shows the name of the person whose data is in the file. (This is the name you typed when the database was first created.) You can change this name at any time by choosing the Settings command in the Options menu. See Chapter 10, *Customizing Personal RecordKeeper*.

The next section of the Status Bar shows the number of Entries in the current Subcategory. This information is also displayed in the center of the Toolbar. Double-clicking on this part of the Status Bar brings up a list of the Entries for the current Subcategory, in their current sort order. See Chapter 6, *Organizing and Retrieving Your Information*.

The third section of the Status Bar shows the first line of the first field of the current Entry. Double-clicking on this part of the Status Bar brings up a list of the

Entries for the current Subcategory, sorted by the first line of the first field. See Chapter 6, *Organizing and Retrieving Your Information.*

The last section of the status bar on the right displays the date on which the current entry was last modified. Versions of *Personal RecordKeeper* prior to version 4.0 did not retain information about when an entry was last modified. Therefore, when a version 2 or 3 data file is converted, all entries will have the date that the file was converted.

## The Menus

Here is a brief description of the menus of *Personal RecordKeeper.*

### File Menu

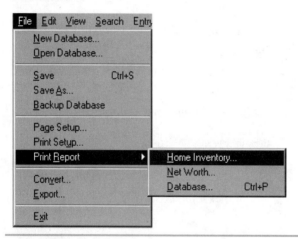

| Choose... | To... |
| --- | --- |
| **New Database** | Create a new database for entering records. Generally you need only one database per person. |
| **Open Database** | Open a previously created database. |
| **Save** | Save the currently opened database to disk. |
| **Save As** | Save the current database with a different name or to a different location on your disk. |
| **Backup Database** | Save a backup copy of the current database file. |
| **Page Setup** | Set margins, font and formatting options of printed reports. |
| **Print Setup** | Change settings for your selected printer, including paper orientation and scaling. |
| **Print Report/Home Inventory** | Print or display a summary of Category 10 Home Inventory. |
| **Print Report/Net Worth** | Print or view a summary of your Net Worth. |

| | |
|---|---|
| **Print Report/Names List** | Print or view a summary of all persons, organizations and business entities names in your Database. |
| **Print Report/Database** | Print all or part of your Database. |
| **Convert** | Convert a database created with an older version of *PRK*. |
| **Import Names/Import WillMaker Names** | Import personal information from Nolo's WillMaker 7 into your Database |
| **Import Names/Import names from other applications** | Import personal information from other applications into your Database |
| **Export** | Export reports or database information from your database. |
| **Exit (Windows only)** | Quit the application and save your data. |
| **Quit (Macintosh only)** | Quit the application and save your data. |

## Edit Menu

| Choose... | To... |
|---|---|
| **Undo** | Undo the last edit in the current Entry. |
| **Cut** | Move the currently selected text to the clipboard for later pasting elsewhere. |
| **Copy** | Copy the currently selected text to the clipboard for later pasting elsewhere. |
| **Paste** | Paste the contents of the clipboard at the current cursor location. |
| **Paste Date** | Paste the current date at the current cursor location. |
| **Delete** | Delete the currently selected text without replacing existing clipboard contents. |
| **Select All** | Select all text in the field in which the cursor is currently flashing. |

## View Menu

| Choose... | To... |
| --- | --- |
| **Toolbar** | Show or hide the toolbar at the top of the application window. |
| **Status Bar** | Show or hide the status bar at the bottom of the application window. |
| **Net Worth Indicators** | Show or hide dollar sign icons on all Categories and Subcategories that are used in Net Worth Reports. (See Chapter 7.) |
| **Empty Subcategories** | Show or hide all Subcategories that have no data in them. *Do not turn off this item until you are finished entering data. All Subcategories are empty when you start a new database.* |

## Search Menu

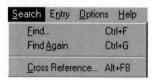

| Choose... | To... |
| --- | --- |
| **Find** | Search for any text within the database. |
| **Find Again** | Repeat the last find request and search further into the database. |
| **Cross Reference** | List other Categories related to the current Category. |

## Entry Menu

| Entry | Options | Help |
|-------|---------|------|
| New | Ctrl+N | |
| Duplicate | Ctrl+F5 | |
| Delete | | |
| First | Ctrl+F3 | |
| Previous | F3 | |
| Next | F4 | |
| Last | Ctrl+F4 | |
| Sort By... | F10 | |
| Go To Entry... | Ctrl+E | |
| Go Back | Ctrl+F7 | |
| History... | F7 | |
| Notes... | Ctrl+T | |

| Choose... | To... |
|-----------|-------|
| **New** | Create a new Entry in the current Subcategory. |
| **Duplicate** | Duplicate the currently visible Entry in the current Subcategory. |
| **Delete** | Delete the currently visible Entry from the current Subcategory. |
| **First** | Go to the first Entry in the current Subcategory, using the current sort order. |
| **Previous** | Go to the previous Entry in the current Subcategory, using the current sort order. |
| **Next** | Go to the next Entry in the current Subcategory, using the current sort order. |
| **Last** | Go to the last Entry in the current Subcategory, using the current sort order. |
| **Sort By** | Set the field on which the Entries in the current Subcategory should be sorted. |
| **Go To Entry** | List all Entries in the current Subcategory, and go to a specific one. |
| **Go Back** | Go back to the most recent screens you have been viewing. |
| **History** | List the last 40 screens you've viewed, and go directly to any of them. |
| **Notes** | Add additional information to the current Entry. |

## Options Menu

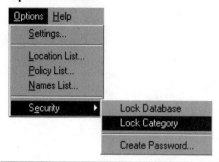

| Choose... | To... |
|---|---|
| **Settings** | Change data entry format warnings, user name that appears in status bar. |
| **Location List** | Edit the list of locations used in Category 10 Home Inventory. |
| **Policy List** | Edit the list of insurance policies used in Category 10 Home Inventory. |
| **Names List** | Edit the list to add or delete names, or enter additional personal information. |
| **Security/Lock Database** | Restrict access to the current file by requiring a password. |
| **Security/Lock Category** | Restrict access to the current Category by requiring a password. |
| **Security/Change or Change Password** | Set a password that can later be used to restrict access. Change a previously created password. |

## Help Menu

| Choose... | To... |
|---|---|
| **Contents** | View a complete directory of online help for *Personal RecordKeeper*. |
| **How To Use Help** | Learn how to use Microsoft's Help System. |
| **Nolo Catalog** | Learn about other products from Nolo Press that you may find useful. |
| **Shark Bait** | Enjoy a little humor when you need a break from entering records. |
| **About (Windows only)** | View version and copyright information. |

## Organizing and retrieving your data

Once you have entered some information into your *Personal RecordKeeper* database, use the following features to organize and retrieve it.

- Look at the Category and Subcategory icons to see where you have entered data.

- Use the Names List to add additional information about persons, organizations and business entities in your database. (See Chapter 5.)

- Import names and related information from *WillMaker* 7 and other address book or personal information manager programs. (See Chapter 5.)

- Use the Hide Empty Subcategories option in the View menu to hide Subcategories you're not using.

- Use the Sort By command in the Entry menu to re-order your Entries. (See Chapter 6.)

- Use the Find command in the Search menu to search for data you've entered. (See Chapter 6.)

- Use the Go To Entry command in the Entry menu to go to a specific Entry in a Subcategory. (See Chapter 4.)

- Use the History command in the Entry menu to instantly return to any of the last 40 screens you've visited.

## Printouts, reports and exporting your data

Use *Personal RecordKeeper's* reporting features to print some or all of your information whenever you want to:

- provide a list of essential information to another person taking care of your affairs while you're away on a trip or in the hospital

- provide a list of assets for your lawyer or yourself before sitting down to prepare a will or living trust

- provide supporting documentation when filing an insurance claim, or

- simply have access to your information when you can't be at a computer.

*Personal RecordKeeper* offers four kinds of reports. You can print out any or all of the data you've entered, or generate itemized or summary reports of your personal information (Names List), Net Worth or Home Inventory. (See Chapter 7.)

*Personal RecordKeeper* also lets you export your data in a variety of formats, which can be imported directly into address book or personal information manager applications like *Outlook*, *Ecco* or *Sidekick*, and *Quicken*, the popular home-finance software. (See Chapters 5 and 8.)

# Chapter 4. Entering and Saving Information

This chapter explains how to enter information, including how to:

- find the right Subcategory for the information you want to enter

- create multiple Entries in any Subcategory

- move from screen to screen within an Entry, and

- attach Notes to any Entry.

You'll also learn about a few of the special features of *Personal RecordKeeper*, including:

- how to enter dollar amounts and dates in specially formatted fields, and

- how to use the lists of locations and insurance policies that are used in Category 10, Home Inventory.

If you haven't yet read the overview of *Personal RecordKeeper* in Chapter 3, do so now. It will help you become familiar with the terminology and get an idea of the kinds of information *Personal RecordKeeper* can hold.

## Finding the right Category and Subcategory

Before you enter any information into *Personal RecordKeeper*, browse through the Categories and Subcategories (listed on the left side of the main application window) to see what's there. You can also read the descriptions in Chapter 3 and a list of all Categories and Subcategories in Appendix A.

Whenever a Category is selected, you can also view a list of related Categories that may contain other relevant information. To view this list:

- click the Cross Reference button 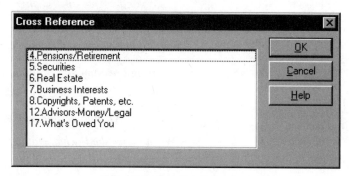 in the Toolbar, or

- choose Cross Reference from the Search menu.

*Cross Reference list dialog box.*

For a description of the relevance of each cross referenced item, click the Help button while viewing the list of cross references.

## Entering information in a Subcategory

Each separate item you record in a Subcategory is kept in its own "Entry." A Subcategory can hold as many Entries as you need.

Each Entry in a Subcategory uses the template that was designed for that Subcategory. This template consists of one to six data screens and is not modifiable. (See Chapter 3, *Overview of Personal RecordKeeper*.)

*Screen tabs on a multiple-screen Entry template.*

When you first enter a Subcategory, a blank Entry is automatically created. You can immediately start entering data by filling in the blank fields. Press the Tab key to go from field to field, or simply click on the field you want to use and start typing.

If the Subcategory template has more than one screen, click on the screen tabs to move from screen to screen or press the Page Up or Page Down keys on your keyboard. The screen you are currently using will be the front-most tab.

## Creating additional Entries

To create an additional Entry, either:

- choose New Entry from the Entry menu,

- press Ctrl+N on the keyboard (Command+N on a Mac), or

- click the New Entry button  on the Toolbar.

When you create a new Entry you'll return to a blank screen (Screen A if this Subcategory has multiple screens). The number of Entries you can have in each Subcategory is limited only by disk space.

EXAMPLE: Felix Slatkin has two checking accounts. So Felix needs to create a separate Entry for each one in the Subcategory *Checking Account* in Category 2, *Available Money.* Felix clicks on that Category and Subcategory, and records information for his first account. Then Felix clicks the New Entry button and enters the information about the second account. The status bar at the bottom of the application window now reads Entry #2 of 2, showing that there are two Entries in the Subcategory *Checking Account.*

TIP: If a new Entry you want to create shares a lot of common information with a previous Entry, you can duplicate the current Entry by choosing Duplicate from the Entry menu. The duplicate Entry provides a new set of data screens for the current Subcategory with the data from the previous Entry already included. You can then edit the fields that differ on the second Entry.

## Moving between Entries

If the current Subcategory has more than one Entry, the toolbar buttons shown below will become active, and the status bar will read "Entry # 2 of 2," or however many Entries there are.

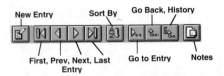

*Toolbar icons after several new Entries have been created.*

 IMPORTANT: Each new or duplicate Entry is inserted after the last Entry, unless you have the Sort feature turned on. If Sort is active, the Entry will be automatically sorted with all the other Entries when you exit the Entry.

You can also go directly to a specific Entry by using the Go To Entry command, which is accessible by:

- choosing Go To Entry from the Entry menu

- clicking the ⬜ button on the Toolbar

- double-clicking the status bar where it says "Entry #: 1 of __"

- double-clicking on the status bar where it shows the first line of the current entry

- typing Ctrl+E (Command+E on a Mac).

Whatever method you choose, a dialog box displays the first line of each entry in the current Subcategory.

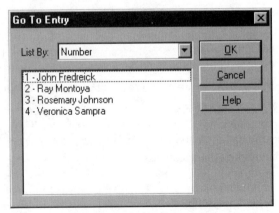

*The Go To Entry dialog box.*

You can list these entries by number, or alphabetically (by the first field of screen A of each Entry). Click on the Entry you want to go to, then click OK.

## Adding Notes to an Entry

If you want to enter information that doesn't fit any of the labeled fields in an Entry, you can include additional Notes by doing any of the following:

- click on the Notes toolbar button  on the Toolbar

- press Ctrl+T (Command+T on a Mac)

- choose Notes from the Entry menu.

*The Notes dialog can be used whenever you need to enter information*
*that doesn't fit in any field.*

Notes for each Entry can hold up to 32,000 characters. When you print out your data, the Notes are printed after the last pre-defined item in the Entry.

When you're done adding Notes, click OK. If you have entered Notes for an Entry, the Notes toolbar button changes from 🗋 to 🗋 indicating that Notes have been added to the current Entry.

 TIP: Do not press the Enter key to exit the Notes screen. Pressing the Enter key simply starts a new line in your Notes text. You can Tab to the OK button and then press Enter to save your notes.

## Making corrections, changes or deletions

To delete anything you type in any field, either backspace over the incorrect characters, or select the text with the mouse, and then press the delete (backspace) key. In addition, the Edit menu has the standard Cut, Copy, Paste, Delete and Undo commands, which you can use.

## Deleting all screens of a single Entry

The Delete command in the Entry menu erases all data from the currently visible Entry only. The program asks you to confirm that you want the Entry deleted. Click OK or press Return to delete the Entry

 WARNING! The Delete Entry command cannot be undone with the Undo command.

## Allowable formats for dollar and date fields

Some data fields that contain dollar amounts or dates require special formatting so that they can be used in computation and sorting.

By changing *Personal RecordKeeper*'s settings you can control how restrictive the program is about allowing incorrectly formatted data in these fields.

Open the Settings dialog box by choosing Settings... from the Options menu.

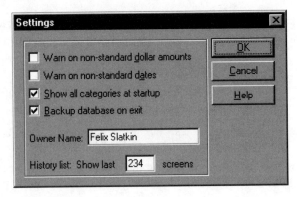

The first two check boxes are labeled Warn on non-standard dollar amounts and Warn on non-standard sates.

- If a box is checked, you will be warned if what you type does not fit the standard a dollar amount (or date) format.

- If a box is not checked, you can enter information in any format.

(For more information on other options in the Settings dialog box, see Chapter 10, *Customizing Personal RecordKeeper*.)

## Proper dollar-amount formats

Dollar-amount fields have the following restrictions:

• they must contain numbers only (text or spaces are not allowed, but $ and commas are okay)

• the number cannot exceed $21,474,836.47.

If you stay within these limits, the program automatically adds a dollar sign and commas when you exit the field. A ".00" will also be added if the amount is an even dollar figure.

Many of the numbers you enter in dollar-amount fields will be used in your Net Worth and Home Inventory Reports. (See Appendix B for a list of dollar amount fields that are included in the Net Worth.) Any dollar amount fields containing text cannot be used in computing your Net Worth or Home Inventory totals.

 TIP: All dollar amounts in *Personal RecordKeeper* should be positive numbers. Liabilities (such as in the Category 16, What You Owe, or the amount due on your mortgage in the Real Estate screens) are automatically turned into negative numbers when your net worth is computed. For more information, see Chapter 7.

If you enter an amount larger than 21,474,836.47, a dialog box will inform you that, "The value you entered is too large." Also, if your total Net Worth or Home Inventory amounts to more than $21,474,836.47, *Personal RecordKeeper* will not be able to compute your total when generating a report. (See Chapter 7, *Creating and Printing Reports*.) But, hey, if you're worth more than $21 million, hire an accountant!

## Proper format for date fields

Dates can be entered in almost any format (see Appendix C for a complete list of acceptable formats); the program will convert them to the Month/Day/Year format. If you type in just the month and day in the MM/DD (number) format, the program will assume the year to be the current year, provided your computer is set to the correct date.

 TIP: You can insert the current date into any field by choosing Paste Date from the Edit menu, or pressing Ctrl+D (Command+D on a Mac).

## Using Location and Insurance Policy lists

In each of the Subcategories in Category 10, Home Inventory, you have access to two special lists:

- Location List, which lists the locations of your possessions, is located on Screen A of every Entry in Category 10

- Policy List, which lists the insurance policies that insure those possessions, is located on Screen C of every Entry in Category 10.

These lists are used in generating Home Inventory Reports. They allow you to sort all Home Inventory items by location or by insurance policy.

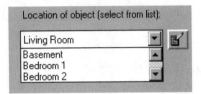

*The Location List appears on Screen A of every Subcategory in Category 10.*

### Pasting information from the Locations and Policies Lists

If you want to enter a location or insurance that's already listed—for example, your rare coins and valuable gems are both located in a safe in your den—you can save yourself some typing by pasting information from these pull-down lists. Pull-down lists are indicated by the triangle icon at the right of the field (see the figure above).

- If the Location of object field (on Screen A) says "No Location Specified," click on triangle icon to pull-down the list and select the location you want to enter. To add, modify or delete items from the list, see *Editing the Location and Policy Lists*, below.

- If the Policy field (on Screen C) says "No Policy Specified," click on triangle icon to pull-down the list and select the policy you want to enter. To add, modify or delete items from the list, *Editing the Location and Policy List*, below.

### Editing the Location and Policy Lists

If you want, you can edit either list by adding, or modifying or deleting items.

### The Location List

When you first use *Personal RecordKeeper,* the Location List contains a few suggested items. To edit the Locations List:

- Click on the list icon next to the Location of object field (on Screen A of any Entry in the Home Inventory Category), or

- Choose Location List from the Options menu.

  A dialog box appears showing what's in the Location List.

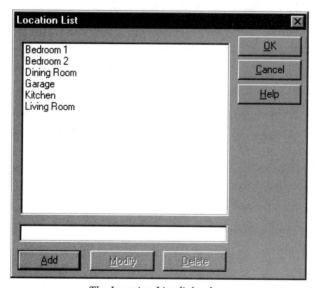

*The Location List dialog box.*

- To **add** an item, simply type where the cursor is flashing and click Add.

- To **change** an item, click on it in the list. This will make its text appear in the editable field at the bottom. Revise the item as you wish, then click Modify. As you add or modify items, they are automatically sorted alphabetically.

- To **delete** an item, click on it in the list, then click Delete.

  Once you have made your list or modified it as you wish, click the OK button.

### The Policy List

When you first use *Personal RecordKeeper,* the Policy List contains just one item, the placeholder "Generic Insurance Policy ABC123." To add items to or edit the Policy List:

43

- Click on the list icon next to the Policy field (on Screen C of any Entry in the Home Inventory Category), or

- Choose Policy List from the Options menu.

  A dialog box appears similar to the Location List shown above.

- To **add** an item, simply type where the cursor is flashing and click Add.

- To **change** an item, click on it in the list. This will make its text appear in the editable field at the bottom. Revise the item as you wish, then click Modify. As you add or modify items, they are automatically sorted alphabetically.

- To **delete** an item, click on it in the list, then click Delete.

  Once you have made your list or modified it as you wish, click the OK button.

## Some tips on using the Location and Policy Lists

- **Keep the items (i.e., locations or policies) short:** Although each location or insurance policy can be more than 100 characters long, it's a good idea to keep them short. Only the first 30 or so characters show up in the list.

- **Any change you make in the Locations List or Policy List affects every Entry in Category 10:** If you delete an item that was selected in a Category 10 Entry, the program will treat that Entry as if no item has been selected.

- **How specific should you make your lists?** Each of these lists is designed to allow you to sort your data when you print out Home Inventory Reports. Accordingly, the specificity of your lists will depend on how specific you want your report's sorting ability to be.

  If you would like to generate a report that is sorted by what is in each room in your house, then list each room in your Location List.

  On the other hand, if you have several houses and just want reports of what's in each house, you would list only the addresses of your various homes. You should also list any other place you keep property (for example, your safe-deposit box).

  In your Policy List you should list separately any extra coverage, "riders" or "endorsements" that you have added to your basic homeowner's policy. That way, when you generate your report, you will be able to tell which items are covered under your basic policy, and which items are covered by the extra coverage.

## Saving your data

*Personal RecordKeeper* has a Save command (in the File menu and the Toolbar), but you generally don't need to worry about saving the data you enter. It's done automatically whenever you switch to a new Subcategory or Entry. All data is saved to the file you specified when you first created or converted your database.

## When to use the Save As command

The Save As command in the File menu can be used to rename a file, or save it in a different location on your hard disk. When you use this command, the new file becomes the current file and the original file is closed.

## When to use the Backup Database command

The Backup Database command in the File menu can be used to save a backup copy of the current database. The file is saved in the same directory as the current file, with the same name except for a BAK extension instead of PR5.

You can also choose the Setting command from the Options menu to have a backup copy saved each time you close a file or exit the application. See Chapter 10, *Customizing Personal RecordKeeper.*

4 *PERSONAL RECORDKEEPER* USER'S GUIDE

# Chapter 5.  Using the Names List

*Entering names and related information*

*Other ways to add  names to the Names List*

*Modifying names and adding information*

*Deleting names from the Names List*

*Importing names information from other programs*

*Other uses for Names List information*

All the names you enter into your *RecordKeeper* database—names of people, organizations, business entities, etc.—are stored in a master Names List. The Names List serves two important purposes in *RecordKeeper*:

- It allows you to easily reuse a name in multiple places without having to retype it each time.

- It stores the addresses, phone numbers and e-mail addresses for each name in your database.

This chapter tells you how to use the Names List to:

- enter the same name in many places without retyping

- add and modify address, phone and e-mail information for each name, and

- import names and addresses from Nolo Press's *WillMaker 7* or from any other address book software you use.

 TIP: To learn how Names List information in is used in printed reports, see Chapter 7. To learn how to export Names List information to other programs, see Chapter 8.

## Entering names and related information

As you use *RecordKeeper*, you will be entering many different types of information into each Entry—including names of people, businesses, banks, insurance companies, etc. For example, on the Entry screens for Category 11. Insurance, Subcategory "Life," you're asked to enter the names of the insured, the insurance company, the policy's beneficiaries, your broker and brokerage company in separate name fields.

Each name field is a drop-down list, as indicated by the down arrow (or upside-down triangle) at the right edge of the field, and has a yellow card file icon to just the right.

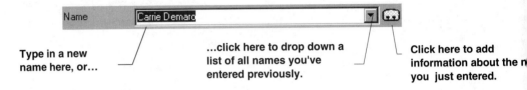

| Name | Carrie Demaro | ▼ | 🗄 |

Type in a new name here, or...

...click here to drop down a list of all names you've entered previously.

Click here to add information about the n you just entered.

Wherever you see a field that looks like this, it means you can enter a name by one of three methods:

- typing it in as you would information into any other field
- selecting it from the field's drop down list of names that you entered previously, or
- pasting it from the Names List dialog.

NOTE: If you are using the program for the first time, the Names List will be "empty" until you have entered at least one name into an Entry or have imported names into *RecordKeeper* from another program (see below). Users of previous versions of *RecordKeeper* who have converted their version 3.0 or version 4.0 database to this version will find that all of the names they previously entered are already stored and sorted in the Names List, and the addresses and phone numbers are attached to the correct name.

## Typing in a name

You can type names into name fields as you would information into any other field. If you're entering a new name for the first time, this is the only way to do it.

After you enter a new name for the first time, we recommend that you enter additional information about that name before you continue to enter other data in the current screen. To do this, click the yellow card file icon to the right of the field you just completed. This will open a dialog in which you can enter more information about the name you just entered. See *Modifying names and adding information*, below.

## Selecting a name from the field's drop-down list

Another way to enter a name in a name field is to select it from the field's drop-down list. To drop-down the list of names you've entered previously:

- click the triangle icon at the right edge of any name field, or
- simultaneously press the Alt and the Down Arrow keys on your keyboard.

The names are listed alphabetically by first name. If the list of names is long, scroll through them by clicking on the scroll bar; or type the first few letters of a name you're looking for and the list will jump to the closest match.

When you find the name you want, click on it to insert it into the name field. (You can also select a name by pressing the Down Arrow key on your keyboard until it is highlighted, and then pressing the Enter key.) If a name was already in the field, the name you select will replace it. You can enter only one name per field.

Once you've entered a name, be sure to add the address, phone number, or other information about the name by clicking on the yellow card file icon just to the right of the name field. See *Modifying names and adding more information*, below.

## Pasting from the Names List dialog box

Another way to enter a name you've previously used is to paste it from the Names List dialog box.

You can bring up the Names List dialog in any one of the following ways:

- Select Names List... from the Options menu, or
- Press Ctrl+L (Command+L on a Mac), or
- Click on the card file icon at the right edge of the toolbar, or
- If the name field you want to complete is blank, click on the card file icon just to the right of the field.

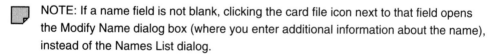 NOTE: If a name field is not blank, clicking the card file icon next to that field opens the Modify Name dialog box (where you enter additional information about the name), instead of the Names List dialog.

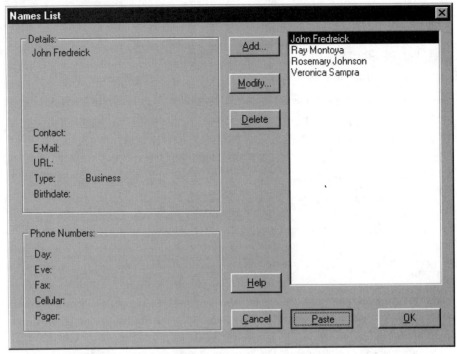

*Names List dialog box.*

In the Names List dialog, the names are listed alphabetically by first name. To paste a listed name into the active field in *RecordKeeper* :

Step 1.     Select the name. When a name is selected, any details you've entered about that person or entity appear on the left side of the Names List dialog box.

Step 2.     Click Paste. This closes the Names List dialog and pastes the selected name into the field the where cursor is currently blinking.

 TIP: You can use this method to paste a name into any field, not just the pull-down name fields.

### Other ways to add names to the Names List

There are two other ways you can add names to *RecordKeeper's* Names List. You've already learned that when you type a name into any name field on any screen, if the name is not already in the Names List, it will be added automatically

The other two ways to add names are:

- Choose Names List from the Options menu, or click the card file icon on the toolbar. This will bring up the Names List dialog of all names. Click the Add button. Then, enter any or all of the requested information. When you're done, click OK.

- Import a list of names from another program, using the Import Names feature. (The Import process is explained later in this chapter. See *Importing names information from other programs,* below.)

Whichever method you choose, the name will be added to the existing names in the Names List and sorted alphabetically by first name. If you added the name by typing it into an empty name field, be sure to add additional information about that name by clicking the yellow card file icon to the right of the field you just completed. See *Modifying names and adding information,* below.

If you attempt to add a name that already exists, the program will not create a new Names List record. Each name appears only once in the Names List.

## Modifying names and adding information

You can add or modify information about a name (such as phone numbers and addresses) or change the spelling of the name by opening the Modify Name dialog.

*Modify Name dialog box*

You can open the Modify Name dialog in any of the following ways:

- Click the card file icon next to a name field that already has a name in it to open the Modify Name dialog for that name.

- Choose Names List from the Options menu, or click the card file icon on the toolbar. This will bring up the Names List dialog of all names. Select the name you want to change, then click Modify or press the Enter key to bring up the Modify Name dialog for that name.

Once the Modify Name dialog is open, enter information into empty fields or edit the field you want to change. When you're finished making changes, click OK.

 IMPORTANT: If you change the spelling of an existing name in the Modify Names dialog, the revised spelling will appear on every *RecordKeeper* screen where the old spelling appeared before. However if you simply type the revised spelling into name field within a Subcategory Entry, *RecordKeeper* will treat this revised spelling as a NEW name and will add it to the Names List. Consequently, the address and phone information about the old name will not be associated with the new (revised) name.

## Deleting names from the Names List

To delete a name, choose Names List from the Options menu, or click the card file icon on the toolbar. This will bring up the Names List dialog of all names. Select the name you want to delete and click the Delete button. If the name is not being used anywhere in the database, it will be deleted from the Names List.

If the name is in use somewhere within your database, program will tell you that you can't delete the name so long as it is still being used. If you want to delete the name anyway, you will need to find *each* place where that name is used and either change the name to some other name or simply delete it. Use *RecordKeeper's* Find and Find Next functions, described in Chapter 6, *Organizing and Retrieving Your Information,* to find each place the name is being used. As you locate each instance, either delete the name from that field, or change the field to some other name, then choose Find Next. Repeat this process until *RecordKeeper* reports that the name can no longer be found. Once you have removed all instances of the name from the database, you can reopen the Names List dialog and delete the name from the list.

## Importing names information from other programs

Earlier in this chapter, you learned how to add names, addresses and phone numbers to *RecordKeeper's* Names List one name at a time. However, if you already have this information stored on your computer in some other program, you can import that information directly into *RecordKeeper's* Names List.

*RecordKeeper* can import names directly from *WillMaker 7,* or any other program that can export names and addresses to a tab- or comma-delimited text file. Most of the popular personal information manager (PIM) programs, such as *Organizer, Sidekick, Act, Ecco* or Microsoft's *Outlook,* can export to these formats.

Once that data is added to *RecordKeeper*'s Names List, you can paste these names in any Entry, or select them from the drop-down list of any name field.

Importing data from other programs can be tricky, so read this section and follow its instructions carefully.

## Importing names data from *WillMaker 7*

Before you can import Names List information into *WillMaker 7*, you'll need to create a Names List export file from *WillMaker 7*. Read your *WillMaker* documentation for instructions on how to do this.

Once the file has been exported from *WillMaker*, follow these steps to import that information into *RecordKeeper*'s Names List:

Step 1.     Select Import Names from the File menu.

Step 2.     Select Import WillMaker Names.

This opens a dialog box which you use to locate the *WillMaker 7* folder and select the file that contains the *WillMaker 7* names list export file. In Windows, the default name for this file is "WMNAMES.WMN"; in Macintosh, the default name for this file "WillMaker Names Export."

Step 3.     Click OK to begin the import process.

Next time you bring up the Names List, the names that were included in your *WillMaker* names file will appear on the Names List dialog box.

 TIP: If you installed *WillMaker 7* to the default folder, the names data export file is located in the *WillMaker 7* folder.

## Importing names data from programs other than *WillMaker 7*

To import names data from a program other than *WillMaker 7*, there are two things you must do:

First, you must prepare the export file from the other program in a format that *RecordKeeper* can use. Then, you must use *RecordKeeper*'s Import Names dialog to tell *RecordKeeper* how to put the incoming data into the appropriate Names List fields. The instructions that follow explain this process in detail.

### *Preparing an export file to import into RecordKeeper*

Address book and personal information manager programs each have their own way of organizing information. For example, *RecordKeeper* has a place for five phone numbers for each name. Other programs may have fewer, or more. *RecordKeeper* stores addresses all in one field; other programs may split addresses into separate fields for Street, City, State, Zip Code and Country. *RecordKeeper* stores full names in a single field while other programs may have separate fields for first, middle and last names.

Because of these differences, you need to prepare the data files you plan to import into *RecordKeeper*'s Names List so that the right information ends up in the right place.

The table below shows the kinds of information *RecordKeeper* can import.

| RecordKeeper Fields | Optional Format for Import |
|---|---|
| 1. Name | *First Name* <br> *Middle Name* <br> *Last Name* |
| 2. Address | *Street 1* <br> *Street 2* <br> *City* <br> *State* <br> *Zip Code* <br> *Country* |
| 3. Contact | *Contact First Name* <br> *Contact Middle Name* <br> *Contact Last Name* |
| 4. Day Phone | |
| 5. Eve Phone | |
| 6. Cellular | |
| 7. FAX | |
| 8. Pager | |
| 9. URL | |
| 10. E-mail | |
| 11. Birthdate | |
| 12. Type (Business or Personal) | |

Note that names can be imported as one, single field (Full Name) or as split-up (or separate) fields (First Name, Middle Name, Last Name). The same is true for the name of the contact person (the Contact field is used if the Name field is a business). Likewise, addresses can be imported as one field (Address) or as split-up fields

(Street line 1, Street line 2, City, State, Zip Code, Country). All other fields are imported as single fields.

The fields in the export file you create from your address book program must match the fields listed in this table. You don' t need to export data that matches every *RecordKeeper* field, but don't bother exporting fields that *RecordKeeper* does not have—there will be no place to put that information.

EXAMPLE: Your address book program doesn't include a field for pager number (a listed *RecordKeeper* field). Don't worry—your export file doesn't need to include all *RecordKeeper* fields. Your address book program, however, includes a field for Social Security Number, which is not a *PRK* data field. Do not include this field when you configure your export file.

To configure your export from your address book or personal information management program, consult the manual or user help that comes with the program you are exporting data from. Look for instructions on how to create and configure an export file and how to export specific fields from that program. Although we can't give specific instructions for every program that you might use, the following general instructions should give you a general idea of the process.

| Step 1. | Open the program you want to import data from. |
|---|---|
| Step 2 | Open the file that contains the information you want to import to *RecordKeeper.* |
| Step 3. | Find and select the program's Export command (consult the program's documentation for the correct menu and command name; usually this type of command is found in the File or Tools menu). |
| Step 4. | Specify the file type of the export file you're creating. *RecordKeeper* can read either tab- or comma-separated (delimited) files. Virtually all programs can export to at least one of these formats. |
| Step 5. | Select the fields in your data file to import into *RecordKeeper*. They should match the list of *RecordKeeper* data fields shown above. If there are fields in the export file that do not correspond to *RecordKeeper* fields, do not include them. If the field order is different from *RecordKeeper* don't worry for now—you'll set the correct field order when it' s time to import the file into *RecordKeeper*. |
| Step.6 | Create the export file. Write down the name of the file and the location where you saved it on your hard disk, so you can locate it when you return to *RecordKeeper* to complete the import process. |

Once you have exported the file from your other program, you can return to *RecordKeeper* and import that file into the Names List.

### *Using RecordKeeper's Import Names Dialog to import the export file*

The next step in importing data into *RecordKeeper*'s Names Lists is telling *RecordKeeper* how to put the incoming data into the appropriate Names List fields. To do this you must first open the Import Names Dialog. Here's how:

- Select Import Names from the File menu,
- Select "Import Names from other program."

This opens the Import Names - Step by Step dialog box shown below.

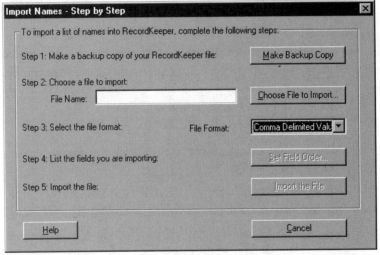

*To import names from other programs, you must complete each of these steps, in order.*

The Import Names dialog lists the five steps required to import the file you just created with your other program. If you have not read the previous section on how to create this file, do so now.

### Step 1.   Make a backup copy of your database

The first step on the Import Names dialog is to make a backup copy. When you click the Make Backup Copy button, *RecordKeeper* will save a copy of your database file with the same name as your database file, except the last three characters will be .BAK rather than .PR5.

DO NOT SKIP THIS STEP! Your backup copy is the only way you will be able to "undo" the names import process if something doesn't go right. For example, if the import is not set up properly, all the phone numbers could end up in the address field. Once the names have been imported, the only way to fix the problem would be to go through each name, one at a time, and cut and paste the information into the correct field—a very tedious process. By making a backup copy of your database, you can simply use your backup copy if the Names Import process does not go perfectly the first time.

 WARNING: If you are attempting to import names a second time because your first attempt resulted in garbled names data, use the backup copy you created in Step 1. For details see *If garbled names data was added as a result of importing a file*, below.

### Step 2.   Choose the file to import

Click the Choose File to Import button to locate and select the export file you created from your address book or personal information manager program. Chances are, this file is in the folder (or directory) where your other program resides.

If you did not read the previous section, *Preparing an export file to import into RecordKeeper,* you should do so now. That section explains how to use your other program to create an export file that you can import into *RecordKeeper.*

### Step 3.   Select the file format

As mentioned in the previous section, *RecordKeeper* can import tab- or comma-delimited files. Select the format of the file that you exported from your other program.

### Step 4.   Set *RecordKeeper's* field order to match the format of the file you are importing

Click the Set Field Order button to open the Set Field Order dialog box. Use this dialog box to match *RecordKeeper's* Names List fields to the fields in the file you are importing.

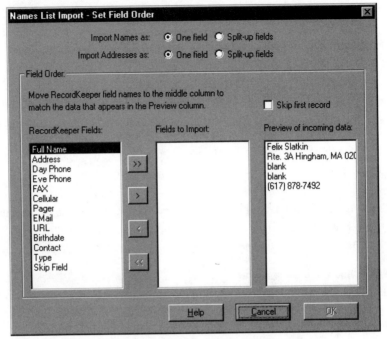

*The Names List Import - Set Field Order dialog box.*

The first thing you must do in this dialog is tell *RecordKeeper* how the incoming file handles names and addresses.

## Import Names as One Field or Split-Up Fields

- If the Preview of incoming data list on the right shows the name split up into more than one line (for example, "John" on one line, "Doe" on the next), select Import Names as Split-Up Fields. Notice that doing so changes the RecordKeeper Fields list on the left, so that three names fields are listed rather than one.

- If the preview list on the right shows the whole name on one line (for example, "John Doe"), select Import Names as One Field.

## Import Addresses as One Field or Split-Up Fields

- If the Preview of incoming data list on the right has an address split up into more than one line (for example, "125 Main St." on one line, "Eau Claire, WI" on the next), select Import Address as Split-Up Fields. Notice that doing so changes the RecordKeeper Fields list on the left, so that five address fields are listed rather than one.

- If the preview list on the right shows the whole address on one line (for example, "125 Main St., Eau Claire, WI 50344"), select Import Address as One Field.

### Field Order lists and buttons

Once you've answered the two questions about how names and addresses are handled, you're ready to tell *RecordKeeper* where it should put each piece of information from the file you're importing.

The Field Order section of the Set Field Order dialog box contains four buttons you can use to match *RecordKeeper*'s data fields (listed on the left) to the import file's data fields (listed on the right):

- The >> button copies all fields in the RecordKeeper's Fields box to the Fields to Import box.

- The > button copies the selected field in the RecordKeeper Fields box to the bottom position in the Fields to Import box. (Double-clicking an item in the RecordKeeper Fields box will also do this.)

- The < button removes the selected field from the Fields to Import box. (Double clicking an item in the Fields to Import box will also do this.)

- The << button clears all items listed in the Fields to Import box.

Here's how to use these lists and buttons to match *RecordKeeper*'s field list.

Compare the list of incoming data (the list on the right) with the list of RecordKeeper Fields (the box on the left). Start with the first line of incoming data. Try to determine what kind of data this is. Then look at the RecordKeeper Fields box on the left and select the *RecordKeeper* field that is the best match for this data.

If there is no matching field in the RecordKeeper Fields list, select the Skip Field item (the last item in the RecordKeeper Fields box). Then, click the > button to move this field into the center box. (You can also simply double-click on Skip Field to move it to the center list.)

 TIP: If you are importing information about businesses, be careful about how you match the *RecordKeeper* fields to your import data. If the import file includes both the name of a business and a contact name, make sure that the name of the business is matched with the RecordKeeper Name (or Last Name) field, and the contact person's name is assigned to the RecordKeeper Contact field(s).

Repeat this matching process for each incoming data field until each data item on the right either is lined up with its matching *RecordKeeper* field, or with a Skip Field item, in the center box.

TIP: If you mistakenly put a *RecordKeeper* field in the wrong order in the Fields to Import box, you can double-click it again in the RecordKeeper Fields box and it will be moved to the bottom of the Fields to Import box.

## Skip First Record

The last thing *RecordKeeper* needs to know is whether it should skip the first record of the incoming file. Some imported data files use their first line (actually, it's the first record) to list the type of data (or field names) included in the file. While this is helpful for matching the imported file to the *PRK* data format, this information does not need to be imported. If the Preview of incoming data box on the right lists field names (like "Name, " "Address" etc.) rather than "real" data (like "John Doe," "125 Main St.," etc.), check the Skip First Record box by clicking it.

When everything appears to be lined up properly, click OK to close the Set Field Order dialog and continue the import process.

### Step 5.    Import the file

When you close the Set Field Order dialog, you should be back at the Import Names - Step By Step dialog box. Click the Import the File button to start the import process.

After the import is done, you're asked if you'd like to view the Names List, which now includes the imported data. We suggest you use this opportunity to make sure that the import worked and to clean-up the new data, if necessary. (see *Viewing, adding or changing information about a name*, above, and *If garbled names data was added as a result of importing a file*, below.)

### *If garbled names data was added as a result of importing a file*

If you find that your first import attempt resulted added "garbled" names data, try it again, using the backup copy you created in Step 1, above. If you try again using your original copy (with the garbled names information), and you make a backup copy of this database, you will overwrite the good backup copy you made on your first attempt, and you'll be left with two copies of the garbled file.

To prevent this from happening, do the following:

Step 1.      Choose Open Database from the File menu.

Step 2.      Set the file type to "*.BAK" to list all backup files.

Step 3.      Select the backup file you just created and click Open.

Step 4.      Now that the backup copy is open, choose Save As from the File menu to save a copy of the backup file as a *RecordKeeper 5* file (so that the last three letters are PR5 instead of BAK).

By giving the file the same name as the original file, you replace the garbled original with the ungarbled backup. Now try the import process again, but be sure make a new backup copy before you import the data.

## Other uses for Names List information

- *RecordKeeper* can create reports of all the information entered in the Names List. For more on how to do this, see Chapter 7, *Creating and Printing Reports*.

- To learn how to export information from the Names List to a file that can then be imported into other programs, see Chapter 8, *Exporting Information to Other Programs*.

# Chapter 6. Organizing and Retrieving Your Information

*Finding information you previously entered*

*Sorting your information*

*Cross references*

*The Go Back command*

*The History command*

This chapter tells you how to search for specific information you previously entered, sort the information and return to parts of the database you visited previously.

To use most of the features described in this chapter, you must have already entered some information into your database file. If you haven't entered any information yet, read Chapter 4 for instructions on how to enter information.

## Finding information you previously entered

### Category and Subcategory icons

As mentioned in Chapter 3, icons in the Category and Subcategory lists indicate where you've entered data in your database.

- Categories with data are indicated by a small piece of paper sticking out of the top of the folder.

- Subcategories with data are indicated by an icon of a piece of paper.

### Hiding empty Subcategories

In the View menu, use the Empty Subcategories item to show or hide empty Subcategories in the Subcategories list. If the checkmark does not appear next to this item, any Subcategories that are empty do not show up on the Subcategory list.

 IMPORTANT: Leave empty Subcategories visible until you have finished entering your data. Otherwise, no Subcategories will appear in the list and you won't be able make Entries for any Subcategories.

## The Find command

The Find command makes it easy to search your database for information you've entered previously. You can search the entire database for, or limit your search to, just a Category or a Subcategory.

You can access the Find command in any of the following ways:

- Choose Find from the Search menu
- Press Ctrl+F (Command+F on a Mac), or
- Click the Find button 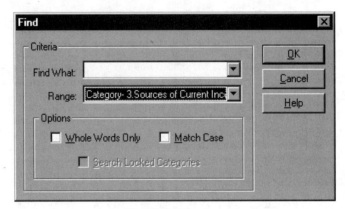 in the toolbar. This brings up the a dialog box shown here.

*The Find dialog box.*

***Find What:***

- Type in the text you want to search for (for example, a specific name, date or amount), or
- Select a prior search request by clicking on the arrow next to the text entry box. You can then select from your last ten search requests.

***Range:***

Select the scope of your search. You can search the entire database or just the current Category or Subcategory.

NOTE: *Personal RecordKeeper* "knows" the current Category and Subcategory, and includes them in the "Range" menu. If no Category or Subcategory was selected before using the Find command (Step 1), you will not be able to choose those options in the "Range" menu.

### Options

- **Whole word only:** If selected, it will only search for the whole word. The search will ignore any instances where the text you're looking for is embedded in a larger word. For example, if you're looking for "*Smith*" it will ignore "*Smit*hers."

- **Match case:** If selected, the search finds only instances that exactly match the capitalization typed in your search request.

- **Search Locked Categories:** If selected, locked categories will be included in the scope of your search. If you haven't entered your password since you opened your database, you will be asked to enter it now.

Searching begins from your current position in the database and stops at the first Entry that satisfies the search request. The program displays the first Entry that meets you search criteria.

### The Find Again command

If your first search request found something that matches your criteria, but wasn't what you were looking for, use the Find Again command to continue searching the database.

You can trigger the Find Again command by any of the following methods:

- Choose the Find Again from the Search menu

- Press Ctrl+G (Command+G on a Mac), or

- Click the Find Again button in the toolbar.

## Sorting your information

As you create additional Entries within a particular Subcategory, each new Entry is kept in the order you created it, unless you choose to sort them.

The Sort By command in the Entry menu lets you sort Entries within a Subcategory based on the contents of any field or combo box. Once the sort feature is activated, new Entries in that Subcategory are automatically sorted as they are created or modified. Each Subcategory can have it own sort criteria. You can change the sort criteria, or "unsort" the Entries at any time.

NOTE: The Sort button only sorts multiple entries in a category, not the whole database. The Sort button will become active when you have more entries (for example, a second car or a second life insurance policy).

To access the Sort By command, select the Subcategory you want to sort and do one of the following:

- Choose Sort By from the Entry menu

- Click the Sort button ![Sort button icon] on the toolbar.

The Sort Entries dialog will appear, offering the following options:

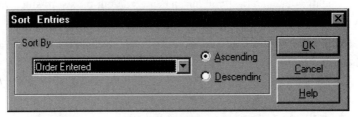

*The Sort By dialog box.*

### *Sort By*

This combo box lists all fields in the current Subcategory. If the Subcategory consists of more than one screen, all fields on all screens are listed.

The default selection is the field the cursor was in when the Sort command was activated.

- To change this selection use the up or down arrows on the keyboard, or click the down arrow and select a different field.

- To "unsort" your Entries, choose the last item—Order Entered. This returns the order of your Entries to the order in which you entered them.

TIP: To quickly select the last or first item in the list of fields, press the End or Home key on your keyboard.

*Ascending/Descending*

These buttons determine whether the sort on the selected field will be Ascending (lowest to highest) or Descending (highest to lowest).

| TYPE OF FIELD | SORT ORDER | |
| --- | --- | --- |
| | Ascending | Descending |
| **Text** | A to Z | Z to A |
| **Dollar Amount** | Lowest to highest | Highest to lowest |
| **Date** | Earliest to latest | Latest to earliest |

Once you've chosen your sort criteria and clicked OK, the Entries will immediately be sorted in that order. New or modified Entries will automatically sort in the proper order as you make changes.

## Cross references

Some *Personal RecordKeeper* Categories are cross-referenced to other categories with related information. This makes it easy to work on all related entries at the same time.

To go from the current Category to a cross-referenced Category, open the Cross Reference dialog box listing the cross references for the screen, by doing one of the following:

- Choose Cross Reference... from the Search menu, or

- Click the Cross Reference button in the Toolbar.

NOTE: If there are no cross references for a particular Category, both the Cross Reference icon and menu command are dimmed and unavailable.

A dialog box will appear, listing other Categories that have information related to the selected Category.

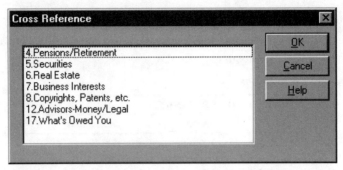

*Cross Reference dialog box for Category 3, Sources of Current Income.*

For more information on how the Categories are relevant, click Help.

To go to a listed Category click it, and then click OK. The Category will be selected in the Category pane (upper left) and the Subcategories for that Category will be displayed in the Subcategory pane (bottom left). However, the main data entry pane remains unchanged until you click a specific Subcategory.

## The Go Back command

The Go Back command returns you to the screen you were just viewing. To go back to the previous screen, either:

- Choose Go Back from the Entry menu, or

- Click the Go Back button in the Toolbar.

If you just used the Find command, the Go Back command will take you to the last screen you were viewing before the Find command was executed. You can keep using this command to go back and retrace your entire session.

TIP: Using Find and Go Back in sequence can make it easy to cut and paste data between two different parts of the database.

EXAMPLE: Sam knows he's typed in the address of Joe's Garage somewhere else in the database. He uses the Find command to search for "Joe's Garage." When he finds the screen containing Joe's Garage, he (1) selects the text from the Address field, and (2) chooses Copy from the Edit menu. Then he (3) chooses Go Back from the Entry menu, which returns him to the screen where he started. He then (4) clicks in the Address field and (5) chooses Paste from the Edit menu to paste the information there.

## The History command

*Personal RecordKeeper* keeps track of every screen you've visited in the current session, in the order you saw them. The History command makes it easy to go back to any screen.

To go back to a screen you visited previously, do the following:

Step 1:      Open the History dialog box by one of the following methods:

• Choose History from the Entry menu, or

• Click the History button in the Toolbar.

Each item listed in the History dialog box contains the following information:
Subcategory number, Subcategory name, Subcategory screen letter, and the first field of the Entry.

Step 2:      Select the screen you want to go to and click OK.

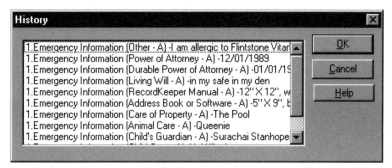

*The History dialog box displays the screens you've recently viewed.*

### Setting the number of items in the History dialog

The Settings command in the Options menu allows you to set the number of items that will be displayed in the History dialog, up to 256 items.

# Chapter 7. Creating and Printing Reports

*Choosing what to print*

*Home Inventory Reports*

*Net Worth Reports*

*Names List Reports*

*Database Reports*

*Printing blank worksheets*

*Previewing a report before you print it out*

*Formatting fonts and other aspects of your reports*

This chapter explains how to generate four types of reports: Home Inventory, Net Worth, Names List and Database Reports. You'll learn how to view, format and print your reports in a variety of ways, and learn how to print blank worksheets.

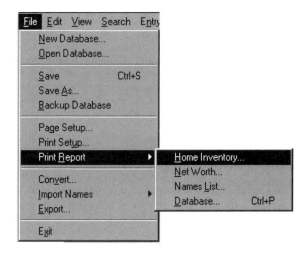

## Choosing what to print

The Print Report command in the File menu offers four kinds of reports:

- **Home Inventory Report:** Generates an inventory of the contents of your home. Use it to compute your insurance needs or to help you file a claim with an insurance company after a loss. This report is based on information you've entered in Category 10.

- **Net Worth Report:** Summarizes all the assets and liabilities recorded in your database and computes your net worth. For a complete list of what fields and what Subcategories are included in your Net Worth reports, see Appendix B.

- **Names List Report:** Includes all fields from the Names List feature (see Chapter 5, *Using the Names List*) for every person, organization and business entity in your database, including address, phone numbers, and contact information.

- **Database:** Includes all fields (including Notes) from some or all Subcategories in your database.

You can display the reports on screen or print them out. You can also export any of these reports. That subject is covered in Chapter 8, *Exporting Information to Other Applications.*

In addition, you can print blank worksheets that can be used for collecting data when you can't be at your computer.

Now let's look at the specifics of each kind of report.

## Home Inventory Reports

Home Inventory Reports total the current value, original value or replacement value of all the items in your home. Home Inventory Reports are based on the data in Category 10, Home Inventory/Valuables. You can only generate a Home Inventory report if you have some data entered in Category 10 of your database file.

This report allows you to estimate your insurance needs, and easily figure an insurance claim if property is damaged or stolen from a particular location.

To generate a Home Inventory Report, select Print Report/Home Inventory from the File menu.

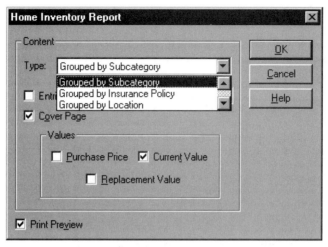

*The Home Inventory Report dialog box.*

The Home Inventory Report dialog will appear, offering you the following options:

### Type:

There are four ways to group your Home Inventory Reports:

- **Grouped by Subcategory:** Lists all items by Subcategory in the order they appear in each Subcategory, with subtotals for each Subcategory, and a grand total at the end.

- **Grouped by Insurance Policy:** Lists all items in the print scope, grouped by the insurance policy entered in the Insurance Policy field on Screen C of each Entry. Subtotals appear for each insurance policy, and a grand total appears at the end.

- **Grouped by Location:** Lists all items in the print scope, grouped by the location indicated by the Location field on Screen A of each Entry. Subtotals appear for each location, and a grand total appears at the end.

- **Alphabetic by Item Name:** Merges all items in the report scope into one alphabetical list, regardless of Subcategory, with a trailing grand total of all items.

  Select how you want the report grouped.

### Entries modified since:

Use this option to limit your report to include only Entries that you've recently added or changed since a specified date.

- To limit the range, click the box and type in the date.

- If you want your report to include everything, leave this box unchecked.

### *Cover Page*

Check this box to print out a cover page at the beginning of the report.

### *Values*

You can print any or all of the three values (which appear on Screen A of each Home Inventory Entry in Category 10).

- **Purchase Price:** This will tell you what you've spent on all your home inventory possessions.

- **Current Value:** This will give you the total value of all your home inventory.

- **Replacement Value:** This is the amount it would cost to replace the items in your home, given the current price for comparable objects if they were bought today. Because insurance policies often cover the replacement cost of lost items, a report that includes this value will help you file an insurance claim.

For each value you include, the report will generate subtotals and a grand total.

### *Print Preview*

Check this option to view how your report will look before it's printed. See *Previewing a report before you print it out*, below.

## Net Worth Reports

Your net worth is made up of:

- **Assets:** The current value of everything you own, plus the current balance on your savings accounts, annuities and the like.

- **Liabilities:** What you currently owe on things like your auto loan, your mortgage and your credit card.

    Appendix B lists all the *Personal RecordKeeper* fields that are included in the net worth calculation. To generate a Net Worth Report, you must have entered data in at least some of the fields listed in Appendix B.

### What's NOT included in Net Worth reports

Items that are *expenses* or *income* are not included in your net worth, because they are considered part of your cash flow, rather than part of your fixed assets. Thus, none of the Subcategories in the Sources of Current Income Category are included in your Net Worth Report—except for the field in the Trust Fund Subcategory where you record the total amount in the trust.

Once you have deposited your income into an account or bought some tangible asset with it—and recorded that information in the appropriate *Personal RecordKeeper* Subcategory—then the value of that asset or account is included in your Net Worth.

## Generating a Net Worth Report

When you're ready to generate a Net Worth Report, choose Print Report/Net Worth from the File menu. You'll then see the Net Worth dialog box shown below.

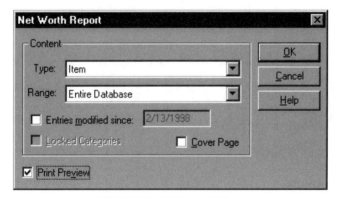

*The Net Worth Report dialog.*

You can generate three kinds of Net Worth Reports:

- **Detail:** This lists your items in Category and Subcategory order—that is, the order in which they appear in the *Personal RecordKeeper* database—and gives a subtotal for each Category and Subcategory.

- **Item:** This report sorts the items alphabetically, by name, and gives only a grand total of your assets and liabilities.

- **Summary:** This kind of report does not list individual items. It gives only asset and liability subtotals for each Category and Subcategory, and a grand total.

### *Range:*

Use these options to select the scope of the report:

- **Entire Database:** Use this option to get your total net worth. Includes all fields listed in Appendix B.

- **Category:** Limits the report to just the assets and liabilities in the Category that is currently selected in the main application window.

- **Subcategory:** Limits the scope to only those Entries in the Subcategory that is currently selected in the main application window.

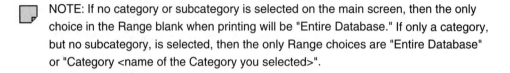 NOTE: If no category or subcategory is selected on the main screen, then the only choice in the Range blank when printing will be "Entire Database." If only a category, but no subcategory, is selected, then the only Range choices are "Entire Database" or "Category <name of the Category you selected>".

### *Entries Modified Since:*

Use this option to limit your report to include only items that you've added or changed since a specified date.

- To limit the range, click the box and type in the date.

- If you want your report to include everything, leave this box unchecked.

### *Cover Page*

Check this box to print out a cover page at the beginning of the report.

### *Locked Categories*

This option lets you include or exclude any Categories you have locked with a password (see Chapter 9). If you want to exclude locked categories, leave this box unchecked. If the box is checked, the locked categories will be included and, if you haven't entered your password yet, a pop-up dialog will prompt you for it.

### *Print Preview*

Check this option to view how your report will look before its printed. See *Previewing a report before you print it out*, below.

## If your Net Worth Report seems inaccurate

If your net worth total seems incorrect, try checking the following things:

*Did you put values in every field?*

*Personal RecordKeeper* computes your net worth by adding the fields listed in the table that appears in Appendix B. Make sure you included values in the correct field for all the Subcategories listed in that table.

If a field is empty, the item won't be included in a report. Also, if there is text in the field instead of (or along with) numbers, that field will not be included.

Check your report for missing items. Use the Print Preview option to display the report on the screen first to save paper. After you're sure the list is complete, then print out a hard copy.

*Is a major item not included in Personal RecordKeeper?*

Check the table that appears earlier in this chapter to see if *Personal RecordKeeper* excludes any items that you would like to include. If you want to include such an item, you'll have to add it separately to the total that *Personal RecordKeeper* produces, or see if you can fit it into one of the Subcategories labeled "Other" that are included in the table.

*Is there text in an asset or liability field?*

If an Entry has text in a dollar-amount field, "N/A" will appear in the "value" column of the Net Worth Report, and the value of that item will not be included in subtotals or in the grand total.

*Does your net worth exceed Personal RecordKeeper's capacity?*

If your total says "$*Overflow*," you have exceeded the *Personal RecordKeeper's* $21 million limit.

## Names List Reports

As discussed in Chapter 5, the Names List contains all the names, organizations and business entities you've entered, as well as related information like addresses, phone numbers, etc.

To generate a report of all the names, organizations and business entities in your database, choose Print Report/Names List, from the File menu.

The Names List Report dialog will appear.

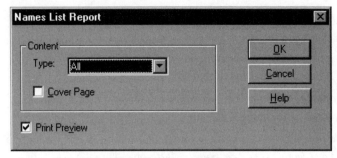

*The Names List Report dialog box.*

Here are the options available for Names List Reports:

*Type:*

You can choose between three types of Names List reports:

- **Personal:** This report lists only the names of persons—names for which you selected "personal" in the "Type" pull-down list that appears in the Modify Name dialog box.

- **Business:** This report lists only the names of businesses—names for which you selected "business" in the "Type" pull-down list that appears in the Modify Name dialog box.

- **All:** This report lists all names in your database.

*Cover page*

Check this box if you want to print out a cover page at the beginning of the report.

*Print Preview*

Check this option to view how your report will look before its printed. See *Previewing a report before you print it out*, below.

## Database Reports

To generate a report of all the data in your database, or just in a particular Category or Subcategory, choose Print Report/Database, from the File menu.

The Print Database dialog will appear.

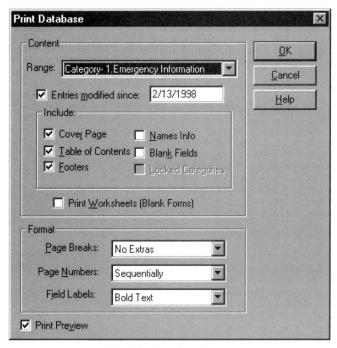

*The Print Database dialog.*

The following options are available on this dialog:

### *Range:*

Choose one of the following options:

- **Entire database:** Prints the entire database excluding Categories and Subcategories that have no data.

- **Selected Category:** Prints all Entries of all Subcategories within the currently selected or opened Category (excluding Subcategories that have no data).

- **Selected Subcategory**: Prints all the Entries in the Subcategory that is currently selected.

- **Current Entry:** Prints the current Entry that is being viewed within the currently open Subcategory. (This menu item is active only when you are viewing an Entry within a Subcategory.)

 WARNING: Think twice before printing the entire database. If your database is large, printing the entire thing can produce hundreds of pages of output.

### *Entries Modified Since:*

Use this option to limit your report to include only items that you've added or changed since a specified date.

- To limit the range, click the box and type in the date.

- If you want your report to include everything, leave this box unchecked.

### *Include:*

To include an item, check its corresponding box.

- **Cover Page:** Prints out a cover page at the beginning of the report.

- **Table of Contents:** Prints out a Table of Contents for your database, by Category, Subcategory and Entry.

- **Footers:** If this option is selected, the bottom of each page will display the date, page number and the name user name (the name that appears on the status bar).

- **Names Info:** Includes personal information from the Names List (see Chapter 5).

- **Blank Fields:** Select this option to include all fields whether or not they have any data. If this option is not selected, fields without data are not included.

- **Locked Categories:** If this option is selected and you have not yet entered your password during this session, you will be asked to type it in now.

### *Print Worksheets (Blank Forms)*

Select this option to print out empty fill-in-the-blank worksheets to help you gather information when you can't be at your computer. See *Printing Blank Worksheets,* below.

### *Page Breaks:*

Use this menu to select where you want *Personal RecordKeeper* to insert a page break (start a new page). The choices are:

- **No Extras:** Starts a new page only when a page is full. This option conserves the most amount of paper, but will make updating your printout more difficult to manage.

- **After Each Category:** Starts a new page whenever a new Category is printed.

- **After Each Subcategory:** Starts a new page whenever a new Subcategory is printed.

- **After Each Entry:** Starts each Entry on a new page. Printing each Entry on its own page uses the most paper, but is useful if you want to occasionally update your report with new or revised Entries. Having each Entry on its own page will make it easier to remove old Entries and insert new ones.

### Page Numbers

Choose from the following page numbering options:

- **None:** Prints data without page numbers. Select this option only if you're generating a short report.

- **Sequentially:** Prints standard, sequential page numbers (i.e., 1,2,3, etc.). Use this format if you plan to print your data only once, and do not plan to supplement it later with updates. If you do plan to keep a printed copy of your data, and plan to add inserts later, use Outline Format.

- **Outline Format:** Instead of using standard page numbers, pages are numbered with the Category number, Subcategory Number, Entry Number and page number for that Entry. For example, page number 27.1.1.3 is the third page of the first Entry of the first Subcategory of Category 27. This format is useful if you plan to keep a complete printout of your data, and want to update it occasionally as you add or delete data. Using the Outline page numbering makes it easy to determine where new inserts should go, and will make it easier to synchronize the printed version with the electronic version on screen.

### Field Labels:

Select how you want the field labels in your report formatted:

- Bold Text
- Red Bold Text
- Blue Bold Text
- Bold Green Text

### Print Preview

Allows you to view how your document will look before it's printed. To print a report while it is being previewed, click the Print button on the Toolbar.

## Printing blank worksheets

As noted above, you can print blank forms as worksheets that can be used for collecting data when you can't be at your computer.

Each worksheet has the name of each field or button prompt, followed by blank lines in which you can write in your information.

By using the Range field of the Print Database dialog, you can print blank forms for just one Subcategory, for all the Subcategories within a Category, or for all Subcategories in the entire database.

To print worksheets for all Categories except a few, lock the Categories you don't want to print (see Chapter 9) and then leave the Locked Categories option in the Print Database dialog unchecked.

## Previewing a report before you print it out

To view how your report will look before it's printed, select the Print preview from the Print Report dialog box. Then, when you click the OK button, your report will be created and displayed on the screen in a Print Preview window.

When you report is displayed, you can use these buttons in the Print Preview toolbar:

- **Print**          Sends the displayed report to your printer.
- **Next Page**      Displays the next page of the report.
- **Prev Page**      Displays the previous page of the report.
- **One/Two Page**   Displays one or two pages at a time.
- **Zoom In**        Displays the report in larger font and is easier to read.
- **ZoomOut**        Displays the report in smaller font and more text per page can be seen.
- **Close**          Closes the Print Preview window.

If you want to adjust the font and font size of the report, close the Print Preview window and select the Page Setup command (in Windows) or the Print Options command (in Macintosh) from the File menu (see *Formatting fonts and other aspects of your reports*, below).

To print the report while it is being previewed, click the Print button on the Print Preview window's toolbar.

## Formatting fonts and other aspects of your reports

To change the font and font size of your Net Worth report:

- In Windows, choose Page Setup from the File menu.
- In Macintosh, choose Print Options from the File menu.

82

To change page orientation, scaling and other printer-specific settings:

- In Windows, choose Print Setup from the File menu

- In Macintosh, choose Page Setup from the File menu.

## Page Setup (Windows)

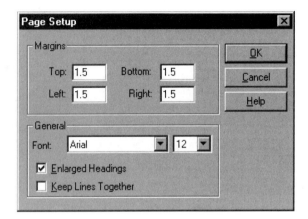

When you choose Page Setup, a dialog box appears with the following choices:

### *Margins*

Type in the margins (in inches) for the top, bottom, left and right of the page.

### *Font:*

Use these pop-up menus to adjust the font and font size of your printout.

### *Enlarged Headings*

When this option is checked, headings for the database and report printouts will print out at the next larger font size from the one selected in the Font Size menu. Turn this off if you are printing with a font size of 14 or larger.

### *Keep Lines Together*

In Net Worth and Home Inventory reports, checking this option keeps the total or subtotal lines on the same page as the Entries they are totaling.

## Print Options (Macintosh)

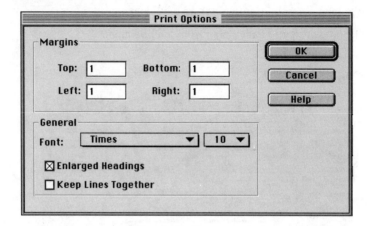

When you choose Print Options, a dialog box appears with the following choices:

### *Margins*

Here you can type in the margins (in inches) for the top, bottom, left and right of the page.

### *Font:*

Use these pop-up menus to adjust the font and point size of your printout.

### *Enlarged Headings*

When this option is checked, headings for the database and report printouts will print out at the next larger font size from the one selected in the point size menu. Turn this off if you are printing with a point size of 14 or larger.

### *Keep Lines Together*

In Net Worth and Home Inventory reports, checking this option keeps the total or subtotal lines on the same page as the Entries they are totaling.

## Print Setup (Windows)

The Print Setup command in the File menu brings up the standard Windows Print Setup dialog box for the printer you are using.

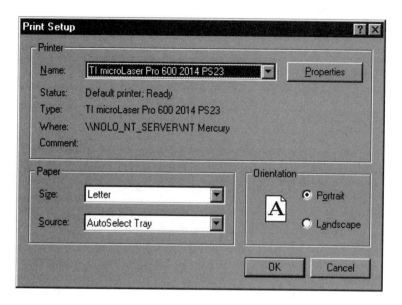

For more information on setting up your printer's options, see your Windows manual or the manual that came with your printer.

## Page Setup (Macintosh)

The Page Setup command in the File menu brings up the standard Macintosh Page Setup dialog box for the printer you are using.

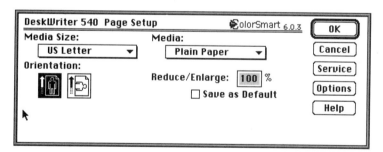

For more information on setting up your printer's options, see your Macintosh manual or the manual that came with your printer.

# Chapter 8.  Exporting Information to Other Applications

*Why export your data?*

*Export options*

*Using exported data*

This chapter explains the various ways to export data from *Personal RecordKeeper* into other applications.

## Why export your data?

Chances are, you'll never need to export the information you've entered into your *Personal RecordKeeper* database. *Personal RecordKeeper's* built-in printing, formatting and report capability will probably handle most of your record keeping needs. However, there are a few reasons you may want to export your data:

- **To integrate *Personal RecordKeeper* data with other applications.**

  ***WillMaker 7*:**  The information in your *Personal RecordKeeper* database can be used to generate Personal Records worksheets in *WillMaker 7*.

  **Personal Finance Software:**  *Personal RecordKeeper's* Home Inventory or Net Worth report data can be exported using "Quicken Interchange Format" (QIF). This format allows you to combine your *Personal RecordKeeper* data with data you may already have in *Quicken, Managing Your Money* or any other personal finance software that supports the QIF format

  **Address Book and Personal Information Manager Software:**  You can also export Names List information into address book and personal information manager programs that support tab- or comma-delineated formats, such as Microsoft's *Outlook* or *Sidekick*.

- **To format your data in ways that *Personal RecordKeeper* can't.** Open your exported file in a word processor and apply any custom formatting you wish.

- **To take advantage of features in your favorite spreadsheet or database program.** Using the tab- or a comma-separated export format, you can import your data into a spreadsheet or database program, and then create charts, graphs or custom reports of your *Personal RecordKeeper* data.

## Export options

To export *Personal RecordKeeper* data in any format, choose Export from the File menu. The Export dialog will appear.

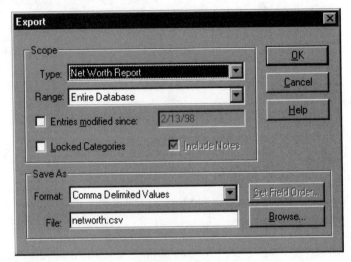

*The Export dialog.*

Here is a complete description of each Export option:

*Type:*

*Personal RecordKeeper* can exports four types of reports:

- **Database:** Includes all fields (including Notes) from some or all Subcategories from any part of the database.

  NOTE: Before you create a Database report, read the section *Using exported data*, at the end of this chapter.

- **Net Worth Report:** Includes only information found in Net Worth Reports. (See Chapter 7 and Appendix B for a complete discussion of what's included in Net Worth Reports.)

- **Home Inventory Report:** Includes only information found in Home Inventory Reports. (See Chapter 7 for a complete discussion of what's included in Home Inventory Reports.)

- **Names List:** Includes information about persons, organizations and business entities included in your database. (See Chapters 5 and 7 for a complete discussion of the Names List.)

If you select Net Worth or Home Inventory Reports and click OK, a second dialog will appear after you exit this dialog. This dialog is discussed in *Additional options for exported Net Worth and Home Inventory Reports*, below.

### Range:

Here is where you select how much data you want to export:

- **Entire Database:** Exports all Categories and Subcategories that are included in the report type.

  For a *Database* report, this includes all Categories and Subcategories that have data.

  If you are exporting a Net Worth Report, this includes all Categories and Subcategories listed in Appendix B.

  If you are exporting the Home Inventory Report, this option is not available. Home Inventory data exists only in Category 10.

- **Current Category:** Exports only the data from the Category that is currently selected in the main window. (If you are doing a Home Inventory report, this option is not available. Home Inventory data is contained only in Category 10.)

- **Current Subcategory:** Exports all data from the Subcategory that is currently selected in the main window.

  If you are exporting a Net Worth Report and there is no Net Worth data in the selected Subcategory, this option will not be available.

  Because Home Inventory Reports include only Category 10, this option is available only if a specific Subcategory of Category 10 is selected in the main application window.

### Entries modified since:

Use this option to limit your export to include only Entries that you've added or changed since a specified date. If you don't want to limit the report in this way, leave this box unchecked.

### Locked Categories

This option lets you include or exclude any Categories you have locked with a password (see Chapter 9). If you want to exclude locked categories, leave this box unchecked. If the box is checked, the locked categories will be included and, if you haven't entered your password yet, a pop-up dialog will prompt you for it.

### Include Notes

This option lets you include any Notes you have added to Entries in the database. This option is not available if you are exporting a Net Worth or Home Inventory Report (Notes are excluded from these reports).

### Format:

Here is where you choose among the data formats for your data. *Personal RecordKeeper* lets you save your exported data in one of four formats:

- **Tab-delimited values (TAB):** In this format, each field (column) is separated by a tab, and the end of each Entry (row) is marked with a carriage return. Carriage returns within fields are converted to a "vertical tab" (ASCII character number 11). The first line of the exported file consists of the field names in quotes, separated by tabs.

- **Comma-delimited values (CSV):** This format is the same as the tab-separated file described above except that: (1) commas rather than tabs separate each column, and (2) if a field has a comma in it, the field text is placed in quotes.

- **Quicken Interchange Format (QIF):** This format is available only for exports of Net Worth and Home Inventory Reports. The structure of this format is explained in the appendix to the user manual of the personal finance package *Quicken*. Use this format to export to *Quicken, Managing Your Money* or other personal finance software that recognizes the QIF format.

 HOW *PERSONAL RECORDKEEPER's* CATEGORY AND SUBCATEGORY NAMES ARE EXPORTED TO *QUICKEN*: When you export your Net Worth or Home Inventory Report to a *Quicken* QIF file, each *Personal RecordKeeper* Category is turned into a *Quicken* "class" and each *Personal RecordKeeper* Subcategory is turned into a *Quicken* "subclass." (*Quicken* recommends using classes and subclasses when you set up a *Quicken* Asset account.) When you import your *Personal RecordKeeper*-created QIF file into *Quicken,* these classes and subclasses are automatically added to *Quicken's* class list. With this information in *Quicken,* you can generate detailed reports in *Quicken* much like those in *Personal RecordKeeper,* with subtotals for each class and subclass. See the *Quicken* manual for information on how to generate detailed reports subtotaled by "class" and "subclass."

WARNING! The data you entered into *PRK* may not "fit" *Quicken's* requirements. For example, in *Quicken* you're limited to 15-character names, while PRK allows longer names. If your *PRK* data file has names that exceed *Quicken's* size limited, this data will not be included in your Quicken account when you import the file. Please consult your *Quicken* manual to learn about its data requirements for importing files.

### *File*

Here is where you enter the name of the file you want created to hold your exported data. The file will be saved in the same directory as the *Personal RecordKeeper* application. If you want to save it to a different location, click the Browse button and select the location.

### Setting field order for Names List exports

If you are exporting data from the Names List in either tab-delineated (*.TAB) or comma-delineated (*.CSV) formats, the Set Field Order button will become active. Click this button to select (1) which of the twelve Names List fields to include in your exported file, and (2) the order of the fields.

 SET THE FIELD ORDER WHEN YOU IMPORT INTO ANOTHER PROGRAM, NOT WHEN YOU EXPORT FROM *PERSONAL RECORDKEEPER*: The number, type and order of data fields vary from program to program. However, all PIM's let you make the appropriate selections when you import the data you've exported from *Personal RecordKeeper*. Since it's almost impossible to make the correct selections unless you are actually running the PIM's import feature, we recommend that you ignore the Set Field Order button and instead use the default field order format.

After you click the Set Field Order button, you'll the Names List Export - Set Field Order dialog box.

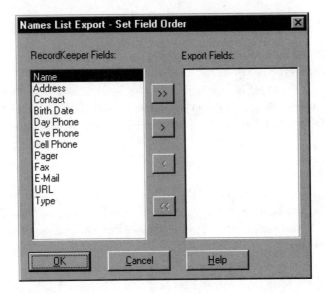

- To export all RecordKeeper fields in the same order listed on the left side of the dialog box, click the >> button, then click OK.

- To export only some fields and set their order:

  1. Double-click on the field you want to include first (this will usually be the Name field) to insert it at the top of the Export fields list on the right side of the dialog box.

  2. Select the next field you want to include first to insert it at the bottom of the Export Fields list, then click the > button.

  3. Repeat Step 2 until all the fields you want to Export are listed in the correct order.

  4. When you're done click OK.

- To remove a field from the Export Fields listed on the right side of the dialog box, select it and click the < button.

- To clear the Export Fields on the right side of the dialog box, click the << button.

## Additional options for exported Net Worth and Home Inventory Reports

If you are exporting a Net Worth or Home Inventory Report, The Export Report dialog will appear after you click OK on the first Export dialog.

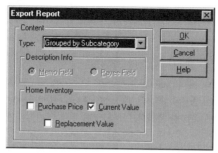

*Additional export options for Net Worth and Home Inventory Reports.*

## Type:

The options offered here are the same as those offered when printing a Net Worth Report or Home Inventory Report. For a complete discussion of these options, see the discussion of printing Net Worth Reports in Chapter 7.

## Description Info

These options are relevant only when creating an export using the Quicken Interchange Format. They refer to which field in the *Quicken* check register you would like the description of your assets to be placed. *Quicken* gives users the option of recording the description of assets in the "Memo" field or the "Payee" field of the *Quicken* check register. See your *Quicken* manual if you need help making this choice. Be aware also that *Quicken* allows only 32 characters per field, so many of your *Personal RecordKeeper* descriptions may be cut short when they appear in *Quicken*.

## Values

Here is where you choose which of the values you want included in your Home Inventory Report (these options are not applicable to Net Worth Reports)

- Purchase price
- Current Value
- Replacement Value.

For a discussion of these option, see *Home Inventory Reports* in Chapter 7.

## Using exported data

This section explains how the various files exported from *PRK* can be used.

## Home Inventory and Net Worth exports

### *Importing Tab- or Comma-Delimited exports*

Because Net Worth and Home Inventory Reports have a uniform structure, you can import them into any database or spreadsheet programs. Consult your software's documentation on how to import Tab- or Comma-Delimited text files.

### *Importing QIF Exports into Quicken*

*Personal RecordKeeper's* exports to the QIF format are designed to be incorporated into a Quicken Asset account, rather than a standard Checking Account. Read your *Quicken* manual for instructions on how to create an Asset account if you don't have one already.

## Database exports

If you make a Database export, keep in mind the following important considerations.

- **Each Subcategory has a different format:** Each *Personal RecordKeeper* Subcategory has a unique structure, designed for the data it was intended to hold. Therefore, the same fields in different Subcategories may be in a different order, and each Subcategory may have a different number of fields.

- **Multi-Subcategory exports will not import properly into database or spreadsheet programs:** If you plan to use your exported data in a spreadsheet or database program, you should export only one Subcategory at a time. Because each Subcategory of *Personal RecordKeeper* has a different number of fields (and spreadsheet and database programs expect every record in a file to have the same number of fields), you will not be able to use multi-Subcategory exports in a spreadsheet or database program.

  The one exception to this rule is Category 10, Home Inventory, in which all Subcategories share the same format and have the same number of fields.

- **Some Subcategories have many items:** The templates used in some Subcategories of Category 6, Real Estate, consist of several screens with up to 61 fields. Some database and spreadsheet programs may have difficulty importing data with more than 32 fields per record.

- **Keep the Blank Fields option checked:** If you plan to import your data into a spreadsheet or database, leave the Blank Fields option checked so that each exported Entry has the same number of items. If you skip blank fields, each Entry may have a different number of exported fields.

### *Format of exported Subcategory data*

For each Subcategory you export, the first line (record) will contain the name of each field in quotes, separated by tabs or commas. The Entries themselves contain only the editable text of each field, or the name of the selection in the combo box. For examples of exported Subcategory data, see Appendix E.

### *Exporting more than one Subcategory at a time*

If you export more than one Subcategory in the same file, the beginning of each Subcategory is indicated by seven asterisks, the Category name and the Subcategory name, as shown in this example:

```
******* Vehicles/Boats/Planes — Motor Vehicle
```

After each of these headings, the data within each Subcategory is exported in the same format as if you were exporting only one Subcategory, as described above.

As mentioned earlier, because each Subcategory has a different number of fields, not all records in the text file will have the same number of fields. This will cause problems if you try to import this data into a database program.

## Names List exports

Because Names List Reports have a uniform structure, you can import them into personal information manager programs, such as *Sidekick*, Microsoft's *Outlook*, *Act* or *Ecco*. Consult your software's documentation on how to import Tab- or Comma-Delimited text files.

# Chapter 9.   Locking Your Data

*Personal RecordKeeper's* locking feature protects your database from anyone without the proper password. You can lock one Category at a time, or the entire database. Once a Category is locked, it can't be viewed by someone who doesn't know your password.

 IMPORTANT! This password protection is not impossible to break—no password is. However, the password is encrypted, so breaking it will be difficult. The actual data, however, is not encrypted, so that someone with a file-reading utility can easily read the data in its "raw" form. If you are worried about keeping your information secure, give a printout and the disk to someone you trust, or store them both in a safe-deposit box. There are also data-encryption programs on the market that can encrypt your data on your hard disk.

## Locking a Category

Here's how to use *Personal RecordKeeper's* password protection:

Step 1.     Choose the Category you want to lock by selecting it from the Category pane in the upper left of the main application window.

Step 2.     From the Options menu, choose Security, then Lock Category.

Step 3.    If you have not previously chosen a password, you'll be asked to do so. Type your password in both fields, then click OK.

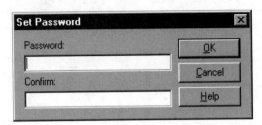

If you already have a password and have not yet used it during this session, you will be asked to enter it at this point.

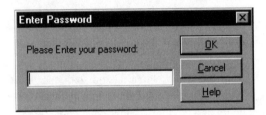

Once a Category is locked, a brown strap with a buckle will appear around its folder. The next time this database is opened, you will have to enter the password to open this Category.

 IMPORTANT! Remember exactly how you typed your password. Spelling, spaces and capitalization must be exact for the password to be accepted. Nolo Press is not responsible for unlocking locked databases.

You can choose only one password for your database file. You must use this password any time you want to lock or unlock a Category or a database.

 IMPORTANT! Once a password is set for the file, it remains unchanged, whether or not any Categories are locked. You will need to remember this password and type it in any time you want to lock a Category, or change the password to something else. The better way to unlock all Categories is to delete the password. (See instructions later in this chapter.)

## Unlocking a Category

The procedure for unlocking a Category is almost the same as for locking one.

If you select a Category that is already locked, the Lock Category command in the Lock menu will change to Unlock Category.

Step 1.    Select the Category you want to unlock. If you have not already entered your password during this session, the program will ask you to enter your password.

Step 2.    Enter your correct password and click OK.

If you type the password incorrectly, you will get a message, "You have entered an incorrect password." To try again, click the OK button and retype your password.

Step 3.    Choose Security, then Unlock Category from the Options menu.

## Locking a database

The Lock Database command, found in the Options/Security menu, allows you to protect your entire database so that the database cannot be opened without a password. If you previously locked only certain Categories in this file, you must use the same password to lock the entire database. If you lock your database, you will be prompted for the password whenever you open it.

Locking or unlocking a database does not affect the status of locked Categories. That is, unlocking a database will not unlock any Categories that have been individually locked.

## Changing your password

The Change Password command, found in the Options/Security menu, lets you change your password. There is only one password for the entire program, so changing the password with this command will change it for the entire database and all locked Categories in the current file.

To change your password:

Step 1.    From the Options menu, choose Security/Change Password.

Step 2.    If you have not already entered your password during this session, the program will ask you to enter your current password.

The old password must be typed exactly as it was originally entered. Any additional spaces, different capitalization or misspellings will be rejected as incorrect.

Step 3.    After you have typed in your old password successfully,  type your new password in both fields, then click OK.

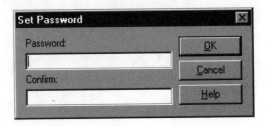

If you have entered and confirmed your new password successfully, your password will be changed.

## Deleting your password

You can unlock the entire database and every Category in the database by deleting the password.

To delete your password:

Step 1.    From the Options menu, choose Security, then Change Password.

Step 2.    If you have not already entered your password during this session, the program will ask you to enter your password.

Type in your password and click OK.

Step 3.    When the program asks for the new password, leave it blank and just click OK.

Step 4.    You will receive a confirmation that all the Categories will be unlocked. Click OK.

# Chapter 10. Customizing
## *Personal RecordKeeper*

*Changing how Personal RecordKeeper appears on screen*

*Changing data-entry and other options*

*Personal RecordKeeper* allows you to change certain default settings of the program, including how the program looks, and how picky it is about the format of dollar amounts and dates that you enter.

## Changing how *Personal RecordKeeper* appears on screen

The View menu has commands to change how *Personal RecordKeeper* appears on your screen.

### *Toolbar and Status Bar*

The first two items of the View menu allow you to show or hide the Toolbar and Status Bar of the *Personal RecordKeeper* window. The check mark indicates that it is visible.

### *Net Worth Indicators*

Some—but not all—Categories and Subcategories of *Personal RecordKeeper* are included in Net Worth reports. (See Appendix B for a complete listing.) The dollar sign icon indicates that a Category or Subcategory is included in these reports. This feature can be toggled on or off by selecting this menu item.

### *Show Empty Subcategories*

If this item is NOT checked, ALL empty Subcategories are hidden. *Personal RecordKeeper* has over 230 Subcategories, covering a wide variety of subjects and property. Chances are you won't be using all of them. After you have finished entering all your data, you may find that you no longer wish to list the Subcategories you aren't using. Uncheck this item to hide the Subcategories you aren't using.

WARNING: If you do decide to hide empty Subcategories, some Categories will appear to have NO subcategories if you are hiding the empty ones. Remember that the empty ones are hidden. You should probably leave all empty Subcategories visible until you have finished entering all of your data.

As noted earlier in Chapter 3, Subcategories that have data are indicated by a "piece of paper" icon next to the Subcategory name. Subcategories with no data ("empty" Subcategories) have no such icon.

## Changing data-entry and other options

Other options are found by choosing the Settings command from the Options menu.

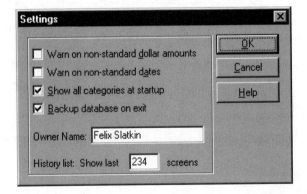

### *Warn on non-standard dollar amounts*

If this box is left unchecked, you will be alerted every time you try to enter text into a formatted dollar-amount field. (See Chapter 4, *Entering and Saving Information*.) If this feature is checked, you can enter anything (text or numbers) into amount fields. However, fields containing text will show up in Net Worth or Home Inventory Reports as "N/A" and will not be figured into any computed totals or subtotals.

### *Warn on non-standard dates*

If this box is left unchecked, you will be alerted every time you try to enter an unrecognizable date in a date field. (See list of allowed date formats in Appendix C.) If this feature is checked, you can enter anything into date fields. However, if you have entered text in this date field, you will not be able to sort it in chronological order. Instead, all improperly formatted dates will be sorted as text and placed after any properly formatted dates.

### Show all Categories at startup

Lets you choose whether you want all the Category Group folders to be "expanded" (to see all Categories) or "closed" (to see only Category Groups) when the program starts up or the database is opened. If this option is checked, all Category Group folders will be expanded, showing all numbered Categories in the Category list.

### Backup database on exit

This option lets automatically saves a backup copy of your file any time you close it or exit the application. The file is saved in the same directory as the original file, with the same name, except for a BAK extension instead of PR5.

### Owner Name:

Use this option to change the name that appears in the status bar of the *Personal RecordKeeper* window, and on printouts of data from this database.

### History list: Show last __ screens

This option lets you set the number of screens that appear in the History dialog when you choose History from the Entry menu. You can set this number as high as 256. For more on using the History command, see Chapter 6.

# Chapter 11. Troubleshooting

*Specifications*

*Frequently asked questions*

*Contacting Nolo Technical Support*

*Nolo Customer Service*

This chapter covers technical information, including limits for data handling and problems you might come across when using *Personal RecordKeeper*.

## Specifications

### Windows system requirements

- **Operating System:** Windows 95 or higher

- **Processor:** 486 or higher

- **RAM:** at least 4 MB

- **Disk Space:** at least 4 MB free.

### Macintosh system requirements

- **Operating System:** Macintosh System 7.0 or higher

- **Processor:** 68030 or higher (68040 or higher recommended)

- **RAM:** at least 8 MB

- **Disk Space:** at least 7 MB free.

### Product specifications

- **Database file size:** Variable, ranging from 64K (empty) up to available disk space. Normal use will result in a database file of about 100 to 600K.

- **Categories:** 27 (fixed)

- **Subcategories:** 230 (fixed)

- **Total number of data-entry screens:** 397 (fixed)

- **Entries per Subcategory:** limited only by disk space.

- **Characters per field:** 1000

- **Characters per Notes screen:** 32,000
- **User defined lists (Location/Insurance):** 50 items per list. Each item can be up to 255 characters (however, only the first 30 or so will appear on the screen)
- **Password:** 24 characters
- **User Name:** 27 characters.

## Frequently asked questions

This section covers problems that may occur as you use *Personal RecordKeeper*.

### When printing a Home Inventory or Net Worth Report, why does "N/A" appear in various fields?

When *Personal RecordKeeper* generates a report, there are certain fields that must contain "real" numbers. If these fields are empty, or contain text, "N/A" will appear in that part of the report. A common mistake is to type a comma in the number. If you do this, the number will be treated as text, and N/A will appear in any reports that include that field.

See Chapter 4, *Entering and Saving Information* for a description of the proper format for dollar amount fields. See also Chapter 7, *Creating and Printing Reports,* for a table of what Subcategories and fields are included in *Personal RecordKeeper's* Net Worth reports.

### Why does "N/A" appear in a Net Worth Report for Vehicles and Real Estate?

In Category 6, Real Estate, most Subcategories have places for a first and second mortgage on the property. In Category 9, most Subcategories have a place for the vehicle loan. If you have entered a value for the property itself, but have not entered an amount for the loan(s) or the name of the lender(s), then N/A will appear where the loan information is supposed to appear.

If you have no loans on an item in these Categories, you can type "No Loan" in the "Lending Institution" field, and type a zero (0) in the "Loan Balance" field.

### Why is the CD-ROM drive containing the *Personal RecordKeeper* disk "inaccessible"?

If you receive a message that the CD-ROM is "inaccessible" when you insert the original *Personal RecordKeeper* disk, you will be asked whether you want to cancel or retry. Answer Retry. Eject the disk and try reinserting it.

If you receive this message again, then either the *Personal RecordKeeper* CD or your disk drive is defective.

Insert another CD-ROM.

- If it works OK and you don't get the "inaccessible" message, you received a defective disk. Return it to Nolo Press for a free replacement (see below). Include a letter describing the problem and an address where the disk can be sent.

- If you still get the "inaccessible" message, your CD-ROM drive is a defective, and Nolo Press won't be able to help you.

## Contacting Nolo Technical Support

Nolo Press offers technical support to registered *Personal RecordKeeper* users.

Phone:       510-549-4660

Hours:       9 A.M. to 5 P.M. Pacific Time, Monday through Friday

E-mail:      NoloTec@nolo.com

If you have technical questions or problems operating this program, read this chapter before contacting the Nolo Technical Support Department.

## Nolo Customer Service

Phone:       510-549-1976

Hours:       7 A.M. to 6 P.M. Pacific Time, Monday through Friday

E-mail:      NoloInfo@nolo.com

Nolo Customer Service representatives can answer questions on product availability, prices, software upgrades, product features, customer registration, policies, procedures and other non-technical topics.

### Change of address

If you move, please send a letter with both your old and new addresses and, if possible, the mailing code on your *Nolo News* mailing label to:

Customer Service
Nolo Press
950 Parker Street
Berkeley, CA 94710-9867
ATTN: CHANGE OF ADDRESS

### *Defective or damaged products*

If you are a registered user and your disk is damaged or defective, we'll replace it free of charge. Send the defective disk and a brief explanation to:

Customer Service
Nolo Press
950 Parker Street
Berkeley, CA 94710-9867
ATTN: REPLACEMENT DISK

# Appendix A. Complete List of Categories and Subcategories

## Subcategories in each Category

**1 Emergency Information**
People to Notify
Child Care
Child's Guardian
Animal Care
Care of Property
Address Book or Software
RecordKeeper Manual
Living Will
Durable Power of Attorney
Power of Attorney
Other

**2 Available Money**
Checking Account
Savings Account
Money Market Account
Certificate of Deposit
Cash
Traveler's Checks
Automatic Teller
Debit Card
Other

**3 Sources of Current Income**
Employment
Pension
Independent Contractor
Trust Fund
Spousal Support (Alimony)
Child Support
Worker's Compensation
Long Term Disability
Insurance Settlement
Rental Income
Royalties
Dividends
Interest
Annuity
Other

**4 Pensions/Retirement**
Social Security
Public Employment
Private Employment
Military
Union
IRA
Keogh
401(k) Plan
Other

**5 Securities**
Brokerage Accounts
Stocks
Corporate Bonds
Municipal Bonds
Mutual fund
U. S. Notes/Bills/Bonds
Commodities
Other

**6 Real Estate**
Single Family
Vacation Home
Co-op/Condominium
Duplex
Rental Property
Tenant Information
Mobile Home/A Park
Mobile Home/Your Land
Timeshare
Undeveloped Land
Agricultural Land
Boat/Marina Dock Space
Airplane Hangar

**7 Business Interests**
Sole Proprietorship
Partnership
Limited Partnership
Corporation
Joint Venture
Other Business Interest

**8 Copyrights, Patents, etc.**
Copyright
Patent
Trademark

**9 Vehicles/Boats/Planes**
Motor Vehicle
Motorcycle
Motor Home/RV
Boat
Plane
Other

**10 Home Inventory**
Antiques
Appliances
Art
Bedding
Books
China/Pottery
Clothing
Coins
Collectibles
Computer
Crystal/Glassware
Electronic Equipment/TV/VCR
Floor Coverings
Furniture
Furs
Garden/Yard Items
Gems
Guns
Holiday Items
Jewelry
Living Things/Plants
Musical Instruments
Office Equipment
Pets
Photographic Equipment
Precious Metals
Recreation/Camping Equipment
Religious Items
Silver
Sports Equipment
Stamps
Tapes/CDs/Records
Tools/Work Equipment
Window Coverings
Wine/Liquor
Other Items/Miscellaneous

**11 Insurance**
Life
Homeowner/Renter
Medical
Vehicle
Disability
Annuity
Other

**12 Advisors-Money/Legal**
Accountant
Real Estate Broker
Insurance Broker
Stockbroker
Auto Broker
Financial Advisor
Tax Preparer
Attorney
Other - Advisors

**13 People/Services**
Child Care-In Home
Child Care-Away
Animal Care-In Home
Animal Care-Away
Cleaning Person
Gardener
Contractor
Repair Person
Pool Maintenance
Pest Control
Appliance Repair
Vehicle Repair
Memberships
Subscriptions
Other

**14 Tax Records**
Current/Not Filed
Past Year/Not Filed
Filed

**15 Credit Cards**
Bank
Department Store
Gasoline
Other

**16  What You Owe**

Monthly Bills
Rent
Money-Written Agreement
Money-Oral Agreement
Object-Written Agreement
Object-Oral Agreement
Court Judgment
Retainer
Other

**17  What's Owed You**

Money-Written Agreement
Money-Oral Agreement
Object-Written Agreement
Object-Oral Agreement
Borrowed Object
Court Judgment
Retainer
Frequent Flyer Info
Other

**18  Alarms**

House
Vehicle
Business
Boat
Other

**19  Secured Places and Things**

Safe Deposit Box
Post Office Box
Things Needing Keys
Combination Lock
Safe
Access Card/Code
Mini/Public Storage

**20  Hiding Places**

Hiding Place

**21  Medical Information**

Family Practitioner
Specialist
Dentist
Eye Care Provider
Other Provider
Medical History
Immunization
Other Medical Information

**22  Memorabilia**

Photos
Letters
Movies/Videos
Cassettes
Mementos
Other

**23  Personal Documents**

Birth Certificate
Passport
License
Marriage/Divorce
Immigration/Naturalization
Other Legal
Educational
Professional
Employment
Religious
Ceremonial
Military
Other

**24  Personal Information**

Personal Data
Employment History
Education
Military Record
Past Residence
Marriage
Former Marriage
Significant Relationship
Former Significant Relationship
Other

**25  Family Information**

Immediate Family - Living
Immediate Family - Deceased
Ancestor
Other

## 26 Death Plans

Organ Donation
People to Notify
Body Disposition
Obituary/Death Notice
Funeral/Service Details
Burial Insurance
Final Resting Place
Epitaph
Other

## 27 Estate Planning

Will
Codicil
Trust Documents
Executor/Personal Representative
Estate Planning Attorney
Letter of Instruction
List of Assets
Other

# Alphabetical Listing of Subcategories

# Appendix B.    What's Included in Net Worth Reports

The following table lists all fields in your *Personal RecordKeeper* database that can be included in your Net Worth Reports.

 TIP: A few Subcategories have more than one field included in the Net Worth Report. For example, in each of the Vehicles Subcategories and many of the Real Estate Subcategories, there is a place for a loan amount and the name of the lender. These figures are included in your Net Worth Report as liabilities. If there is an amount entered for the value of the vehicle or real estate, but no lender name or loan amount, then "N/A" will appear in the report where the loan amount should be. If you have no outstanding loan balance, you can enter $0 in the loan amount field and enter the words "No Lender" in the lender name field.

 TIP: Notice that in the U.S. Notes/Bills/Bonds Subcategory, the field that is used in net worth is the "Trading at" field, rather than the "Value" field. This is because bonds often have a face value which is different than their actual value. Their actual value is what they would currently bring on the bond market. These figures can be found in the business pages of many major newspapers, or the *Wall Street Journal*.

## Assets (sorted by Subcategory Name)

| Subcategory | Cat. | Field |
|---|---|---|
| **401(k) Plan** | 4 | Balance |
| **Agricultural Land** | 6 | Your equity |
| **Annuity** | 11 | Cash value |
| **Antiques** | 10 | Current value |
| **Appliances** | 10 | Current value |
| **Art** | 10 | Current value |
| **Bedding** | 10 | Current value |
| **Boat** | 9 | Current value |
| **Books** | 10 | Current value |
| **Borrowed Object** | 17 | Value of object |
| **Brokerage Accounts** | 5 | Value |
| **Cash** | 2 | Amount |
| **Certificate of Deposit** | 2 | Usual balance |
| **Checking Account** | 2 | Usual balance |
| **China/Pottery** | 10 | Current value |
| **Clothing** | 10 | Current value |
| **Coins** | 10 | Current value |
| **Collectibles** | 10 | Current value |
| **Commodities** | 5 | Value |
| **Computer** | 10 | Current value |
| **Co-op/Condominium** | 6 | Market value |
| **Copyright** | 8 | Current value of copyright |
| **Corporate Bonds** | 5 | Value |
| **Corporation** | 7 | Current value of your equity |
| **Court Judgment** | 17 | Amount |
| **Crystal/Glassware** | 10 | Current value |
| **Duplex** | 6 | Market value |
| **Electronic Equip/TV/VCR** | 10 | Current value |
| **Floor Coverings** | 10 | Current value |
| **Furniture** | 10 | Current value |
| **Furs** | 10 | Current value |
| **Garden/Yard Items** | 10 | Current value |

| Subcategory | Cat. | Field |
|---|---|---|
| **Gems** | 10 | Current value |
| **Guns** | 10 | Current value |
| **Holiday Items** | 10 | Current value |
| **IRA** | 4 | Balance |
| **Jewelry** | 10 | Current value |
| **Joint Venture** | 7 | Current equity |
| **Keogh** | 4 | Balance |
| **Life (Insurance)** | 11 | Cash surrender value |
| **Limited Partnership** | 7 | Current equity |
| **Living Things/Plants** | 10 | Current value |
| **Mobile Home/Your Land** | 6 | Market value of home |
| **Mobile Home/Your Land** | 6 | Market value of land |
| **Mobile Home/A Park** | 6 | Market value of home |
| **Money Market Account** | 2 | Usual balance |
| **Money—Oral Agreement (What's Owed You)** | 17 | Amount |
| **Money—Written Agreement (What's Owed You)** | 17 | Amount |
| **Motor Vehicle** | 9 | Current value |
| **Motor Home/RV** | 9 | Current value |
| **Municipal Bonds** | 5 | Value |
| **Musical Instruments** | 10 | Current value |
| **Mutual Fund** | 5 | Value |
| **Object—Oral Agreement (What's Owed You)** | 17 | Value of object |
| **Object—Written Agreement (What's Owed You)** | 17 | Value of object |
| **Office Equipment** | 10 | Current value |
| **Other—Available Money** | 2 | Usual balance |
| **Other—Business Interest** | 7 | Value of your equity |
| **Other—Insurance** | 11 | Cash value |

| Subcategory | Cat. | Field |
|---|---|---|
| Other—Items/Miscellaneous | 10 | Current value |
| Other—Motor Vehicle | 9 | Current value |
| Other—Securities | 5 | Value |
| Partnership | 7 | Your equity value |
| Patent | 8 | Current value of patent |
| Pets | 10 | Current value |
| Photographic Equipment | 10 | Current value |
| Plane | 9 | Current value |
| Precious Metal | 10 | Current value |
| Recreation/Camping Equip. | 10 | Current value |
| Religious Items | 10 | Current value |
| Rental Property | 6 | Market value |
| Savings Account | 2 | Usual balance |
| Silver | 10 | Current value |

| Subcategory | Cat. | Field |
|---|---|---|
| Single Family | 6 | Market value |
| Sole Proprietorship | 7 | Value of your equity |
| Sports Equipment | 10 | Current value |
| Stamps | 10 | Current value |
| Stocks | 5 | Value |
| Tapes/CDs/Records | 10 | Current value |
| Tools/Work Equipment | 10 | Current value |
| Traveler's Checks | 2 | Amount |
| Trust Fund | 3 | Total in trust |
| U. S. Notes/Bills/Bonds | 5 | Trading at |
| Undeveloped Land | 6 | Market value |
| Vacation Home | 6 | Market value |
| Wine/Liquor | 10 | Current value |

## Liabilities (sorted by Subcategory Name)

| Subcategory | Cat. | Field |
|---|---|---|
| Bank (Credit Card) | 15 | Usual balance |
| Boat | 9 | Loan balance |
| Co-op/Condominium (1st) | 6 | 1st mortgage total |
| Co-op/Condominium (2nd) | 6 | 2nd mortgage total |
| Court Judgment | 16 | Amount |
| Department Store (Credit Card) | 15 | Usual balance |
| Duplex (1st) | 6 | 1st mortgage total |
| Duplex (2nd) | 6 | 2nd mortgage total |
| Gasoline (Credit Card) | 15 | Usual balance |
| Mobile Home/A Park | 6 | Loan balance |
| Mobile Home/Your Land | 6 | Loan balance |
| Money—Oral Agreement (What You Owe) | 16 | Amount |
| Money—Written Agreement (What You Owe) | 16 | Amount |
| Motorcycle | 9 | Loan balance |

| Subcategory | Cat. | Field |
|---|---|---|
| Motor Home/RV | 9 | Loan balance |
| Object—Oral Agreement (Loan) | 16 | Value of object |
| Object—Written Agreement (Loan) | 16 | Value of object |
| Other—Credit Card | 15 | Usual balance |
| Other—Motor Vehicle | 9 | Loan balance |
| Plane | 9 | Loan balance |
| Rental Property (1st) | 6 | 1st mortgage total |
| Rental Property (2nd) | 6 | 2nd mortgage total |
| Single Family (1st) | 6 | 1st mortgage total |
| Single Family (2nd) | 6 | 2nd mortgage total |
| Undeveloped Land | 6 | Loan balance |
| Vacation Home (1st) | 6 | 1st mortgage total |
| Vacation Home (2nd) | 6 | 2nd mortgage total |

120

# Assets (sorted by Category Number)

| Subcategory | Cat. | Field |
|---|---|---|
| **Cash** | 2 | Amount |
| **Certificate of Deposit** | 2 | Usual balance |
| **Checking Account** | 2 | Usual balance |
| **Money Market Account** | 2 | Usual balance |
| **Other—Available Money** | 2 | Usual balance |
| **Savings Account** | 2 | Usual balance |
| **Traveler's Checks** | 2 | Amount |
| **Trust Fund** | 3 | Total in trust |
| **401(k) Plan** | 4 | Balance |
| **IRA** | 4 | Balance |
| **Brokerage Accounts** | 5 | Value |
| **Corporate Bonds** | 5 | Value |
| **Municipal Bonds** | 5 | Value |
| **Commodities** | 5 | Value |
| **Mutual Fund** | 5 | Value |
| **Other—Securities** | 5 | Value |
| **Stocks** | 5 | Value |
| **U. S. Notes/Bills/Bonds** | 5 | Trading at |
| **Agricultural Land** | 6 | Your equity |
| **Co-op/Condominium** | 6 | Market value |
| **Duplex** | 6 | Market value |
| **Mobile Home/A Park** | 6 | Market value of home |
| **Mobile Home/Your Land** | 6 | Market value of home |
| **Mobile Home/Your Land** | 6 | Market value of land |
| **Rental Property** | 6 | Market value |
| **Single Family** | 6 | Market value |
| **Undeveloped Land** | 6 | Market value |
| **Vacation Home** | 6 | Market value |
| **Corporation** | 7 | Current value your your equity |
| **Joint Venture** | 7 | Current equity |
| **Limited Partnership** | 7 | Current equity |

| Subcategory | Cat. | Field |
|---|---|---|
| **Other—Business Interest** | 7 | Value of your equity |
| **Partnership** | 7 | Your equity value |
| **Sole Proprietorship** | 7 | Value of your equity |
| **Copyright** | 8 | Current value of copyright |
| **Patent** | 8 | Current value of patent |
| **Motor Vehicle** | 9 | Current value |
| **Motorcycle** | 9 | Current value |
| **Motor Home/RV** | 9 | Current value |
| **Boat** | 9 | Current value |
| **Plane** | 9 | Current value |
| **Other—Motor Vehicle** | 9 | Current value |
| **Antiques** | 10 | Current value |
| **Appliances** | 10 | Current value |
| **Art** | 10 | Current value |
| **Bedding** | 10 | Current value |
| **Books** | 10 | Current value |
| **China/Pottery** | 10 | Current value |
| **Clothing** | 10 | Current value |
| **Coins** | 10 | Current value |
| **Collectibles** | 10 | Current value |
| **Computer** | 10 | Current value |
| **Crystal/Glassware** | 10 | Current value |
| **Electronic Equip/TV/VCR** | 10 | Current value |
| **Floor Coverings** | 10 | Current value |
| **Furniture** | 10 | Current value |
| **Furs** | 10 | Current value |
| **Garden/Yard Items** | 10 | Current value |
| **Gems** | 10 | Current value |
| **Guns** | 10 | Current value |
| **Holiday Items** | 10 | Current value |

| Subcategory | Cat. | Field |
|---|---|---|
| **Jewelry** | 10 | Current value |
| **Living Things/Plants** | 10 | Current value |
| **Musical Instruments** | 10 | Current value |
| **Office Equipment** | 10 | Current value |
| **Other—Items/Miscellaneous** | 10 | Current value |
| **Pets** | 10 | Current value |
| **Photographic Equipment** | 10 | Current value |
| **Precious Metal** | 10 | Current value |
| **Recreation/Camping Equip.** | 10 | Current value |
| **Religious Items** | 10 | Current value |
| **Silver** | 10 | Current value |
| **Sports Equipment** | 10 | Current value |
| **Stamps** | 10 | Current value |
| **Tapes/CDs/Records** | 10 | Current value |

| Subcategory | Cat. | Field |
|---|---|---|
| **Tools/Work Equipment** | 10 | Current value |
| **Wine/Liquor** | 10 | Current value |
| **Annuity** | 11 | Cash value |
| **Life (Insurance)** | 11 | Cash surrender value |
| **Other—Insurance** | 11 | Cash value |
| **Borrowed Object** | 17 | Value of object |
| **Court Judgment** | 17 | Amount |
| **Money—Oral Agreement (What's Owed You)** | 17 | Amount |
| **Money—Written Agreement (What's Owed You)** | 17 | Amount |
| **Object—Oral Agreement (What's Owed You)** | 17 | Value of object |
| **Object—Written Agreement (What's Owed You)** | 17 | Value of object |

## Liabilities (sorted by Category Number)

| Subcategory | Cat. | Field |
|---|---|---|
| **Co-op/Condominium (1st)** | 6 | 1st mortgage total |
| **Co-op/Condominium (2nd)** | 6 | 2nd mortgage total |
| **Duplex (1st)** | 6 | 1st mortgage total |
| **Duplex (2nd )** | 6 | 2nd mortgage total |
| **Mobile Home/A Park** | 6 | Loan balance |
| **Mobile Home/Your Land** | 6 | Loan balance |
| **Rental Property (1st)** | 6 | 1st mortgage total |
| **Rental Property (2nd)** | 6 | 2nd mortgage total |
| **Single Family (1st)** | 6 | 1st mortgage total |
| **Single Family (2nd)** | 6 | 2nd mortgage total |
| **Undeveloped Land** | 6 | Loan balance |
| **Vacation Home (1st)** | 6 | 1st mortgage total |
| **Vacation Home (2nd)** | 6 | 2nd mortgage total |
| **Motor Vehicle** | 9 | Loan balance |
| **Motorcycle** | 9 | Loan balance |
| **Motor Home/RV** | 9 | Loan balance |

| Subcategory | Cat. | Field |
|---|---|---|
| **Boat** | 9 | Loan balance |
| **Plane** | 9 | Loan balance |
| **Other—Motor Vehicle** | 9 | Loan balance |
| **Bank (Credit Card)** | 15 | Usual balance |
| **Department Store (Credit Card)** | 15 | Usual balance |
| **Gasoline (Credit Card)** | 15 | Usual balance |
| **Other—Credit Card** | 15 | Usual balance |
| **Court Judgment** | 16 | Amount |
| **Money—Oral Agreement (Loan)** | 16 | Amount |
| **Money—Written Agreement (What's Owed You)** | 16 | Amount |
| **Object—Oral Agreement (What's Owed You)** | 16 | Value of object |
| **Object—Written Agreement (What's Owed You)** | 16 | Value of object |

# Appendix C.    Formats for Entering Dates

| FORMATS FOR DATE FIELDS | |
|---|---|
| Allowed<br>(will be saved as "real" dates and<br>converted to MM/DD/YYYY format when<br>you exit the screen) | Not allowed<br>(will be saved as text, or will not be<br>allowed if "Flexible dates" is not checked<br>in Preferences dialog box) |
| March 4, 1998 | March 4 |
| March 4, 98 | March 4, '98 |
| Mar 4, 1998 | March 98 |
| Mar 4 98 | March 1998 |
| 3/4/1998 | 3/98 |
| 3/4/98 | 3/1998 |
| 3/4 | 3-98 |
| 3-4-1998 | 3-1998 |
| 3-4-98 | |
| 3-4 | |
| 3 4 1998 | |
| 3 4 98 | |
| 3 4 | |

# Appendix D.    Keyboard Shortcuts

 MAC USERS! Substitute the Command key (that's the key with the Apple icon to the left of the Space bar) for the Ctrl key.

### Navigating around the screen

| To | Press |
|---|---|
| Move from pane to pane | **Ctrl+Tab** |
| Move to previous pane | **Ctrl+Shift+Tab** |

### In Category or Subcategory pane

| | |
|---|---|
| Select next item | **Down arrow** |
| Select previous item | **Up arrow** |
| Select first item | **Home** |
| Select last item | **End** |
| Select current item & go to next pane | **Space bar or Enter** |

### In Data Entry Pane

| | |
|---|---|
| Go to Next Field | **Tab** |
| Go to Previous Field | **Shift+Tab** |
| Go to Next Screen | **Page Down** |
| Go to Previous Screen | **Page Up** |
| Go to Next Entry | **Ctrl + Down arrow** |
| Go to Previous Entry | **Ctrl + Up arrow** |
| Go to Last Entry | **Ctrl + U** |
| Go to First Entry | **Ctrl + Y** |
| Add Notes | **Ctrl+T** |
| New Entry | **Ctrl+N** |
| Go to specific Entry | **Ctrl+E** |
| Display History list | **Ctrl+H** |
| Go Back to previous screen | **Ctrl+B** |

### Searching

| | |
|---|---|
| Find | **Ctrl+F** |
| Find Again | **Ctrl+G** |

**Text Editing in a field**

| | |
|---|---|
| Next word | **Ctrl+Right arrow** |
| Previous word | **Ctrl+Left arrow** |
| Select next word | **Ctrl+Shift+Right arrow** |
| Select previous word | **Ctrl+Shift+Left arrow** |
| Start of line | **Home** |
| End of line | **End** |
| Next line | **Down arrow** |
| Previous line | **Up arrow** |
| Add Notes | **Ctrl+T** |
| Cut selected text | **Ctrl+X** |
| Copy selected text | **Ctrl+C** |
| Paste selected text | **Ctrl+V** |
| Undo last edit | **Ctrl+Z** |

# Appendix E.    Examples of Exported Subcategory Data

For each Subcategory you export, the first line (record) will contain the name of each field in quotes and separated by tabs or commas. The Entries themselves contain only the editable text of each field, or the name of the highlighted radio button.

EXAMPLE: Subcategory "Photos" in the Category "Memorabilia/Things" has four fields in it:

- SUBJECT

- SIGNIFICANCE OR INTERESTING INFORMATION

- PHYSICAL DESCRIPTION

- LOCATION OF PHOTOS

If there are three filled-in Entries in this Subcategory, a comma-separated export of this Subcategory would look like this:

*"Subject", "Significance or interesting information ","Physical description","Location of photos"*

*Taj Mahal, Taken on vacation to India in 1948.,An 8 x 10 colored glossy photo in an oak frame,On the living room wall.*

*"Great Grandpa Hildebrandt in front of his farm house in Buckley, Michigan in November of 1962.",The only known photo of Great Grandpa.,A black & white snapshot,Page 3 of the brown photo album marked "Hidebrandt."*

*"Joey's first steps, taken on May 9th, 1952.",,B & W snapshot,Blue photo album marked "Joe's family photos"*

If you imported this information into a spreadsheet or turned it into a table you could get it to look something like this:

| "Subject" | "Significance or interesting information" | "Physical description" | "Location of photos" |
| --- | --- | --- | --- |
| Taj Mahal | Taken on vacation to India in 1948. | An 8 x 10 colored glossy photo in an oak frame | On the living room wall. |
| Great Grandpa Hildebrandt in front of his farm house in Buckley, Michigan in November of 1922. | The only known photo of Great Grandpa. | A black & white snapshot | Page 3 of the brown photo album marked "Hildebrandt ." |
| Joey's first steps, taken on May 9th, 1952. | | B & W snapshot | Blue photo album marked "Joe's family photos" |

This table was made in *Microsoft Word 6.0* from *Personal RecordKeeper* data

Notice that each Entry has become a row or "record" and there are four "fields" or "items" in each record.

 TIP: If you are planning to import this data into a word processor in order to make a table, be aware that some word processors cannot make tables exceeding 31 columns. Some *Personal RecordKeeper* Subcategories in the Real Estate Category have as many as 61 fields. Accordingly, you will not be able to use a word processor to make a table of certain Subcategories.

## Exporting more than one Subcategory at a time

If you export more than one Subcategory in the same file, the beginning of each Subcategory is indicated by seven asterisks, the Category name and the Subcategory name, as shown in this example:

```
******* Vehicles/Boats/Planes — Motor Vehicle
```

After each of these headings, the data within each Subcategory is exported in the same format as if you were exporting only one Subcategory (see previous section).

As mentioned earlier, because each Subcategory has a different number of fields, not all records in the text file will have the same number of fields. This irregularity will be a problem if you try to import this data into a database program.

# Index